Malice Love
Diary Of A Mob Hitman

Malice Love
Diary Of A Mob Hitman

Although based on real people and true events, some names and events have been changed out of respect and for dramatic effect. I hope you enjoy it regardless.

Milo caused pain. This was his gift in life. He killed without remorse or regret.

He has been called 'the most evil bastard alive,' as well as 'the devil himself in human form.' Anyone who knew him well – that he didn't kill – would have definitely agreed to the aforementioned descriptions of him.

Milo had learned at an early age that love was malicious. Love was malice and malice love. He had learned this as a young boy, watching his father beat his younger brother to death.

Perhaps, this was why, after all those years later, he still seemed to hold a grudge against the whole world around him. Nobody was safe or immune from his wrath, including his wife, Barbara. He even went as far as to insert a knife blade into her back following an argument, and telling her, as she felt the blood running down between her shoulder blades, that she might as well get used to it. This was the best she was going to get from him as a husband.

Needless to say, she filed for divorce – which, of course, only served to fuel his fury even more.

#

Milo enjoyed riding the ferry over to Manhattan and taking long walks on the dark city streets looking for new victims.

To him, it was almost therapeutic. A way to unwind. And he was actually doing the world a favor, as he saw it. Just another waste of life and breath off the streets. Just one more bum, one more thief, or one more rapist off the street.

He always carried the tools of the trade with him; a .38 derringer, a knife, sometimes an ice pick. He never knew when he might need one of them, there was so much filth on the streets to take care of.

To eliminate. To *eradicate*.

He hated the bums especially. They smelled like walking death and had bad breath and filthy clothes and were always begging for money. And he hated it when they got pushy. And talked *loudly*. Some of them wouldn't give up, would just follow him down the street and keep asking him – almost demanding him – to give them some spare change.

Look at that suit you got on. You can afford some spare change, you rich asshole.

Buzz off, he would say. *Before you get hurt.*

I said, give me some MONEY, the bums would say, not knowing who they were messing with until it was too late.

Milo got real quiet, just standing there giving them that death stare. He was patient for so long, then...when his patience ran out, so did your life.

Before he knew what hit him, the bum had received two quick jabs from Milo's knife blade, both wounds deep and fatal. Within seconds the bum was lying on the ground, gasping for breath, choking on his own blood. Milo just stood over him, watching him die.

He liked watching them die. Seeing the light in their eyes go out. He enjoyed knowing that the last thing they saw before dying was his face, looking down on them, wearing a big grin.

#

He really enjoyed these trips to Manhattan. Plenty of practice in different ways of killing people. He enjoyed the exercise too. To him, this was all the exercise he needed. Killing people and dumping their bodies off a bridge or slicing their guts open with his knife – to prevent any body gases from building up, so if they were dumped in a body of water they would be sure to sink instead of floating to the surface – and watching them die a slow, excruciating death.

He was slowly but surely perfecting his craft.

He was only nineteen years old at the time.

#

Milo was finally *perfecting* the art of murder.

Milo could be the nightmare you *never* want to have.

He can haunt you in the midnight and come after you with an upraised scythe like the Grim Reaper. He can reach out and touch you no matter where you hide, whether you are a pedophile priest or a drug dealer or a wife beater or even the President of the United States.

He can find out what books you read what porn movies you buy, your favorite brand of liquor, or the dosing schedule for your Prozac prescription.

He is the guy who can sign your hall passes from Purgatory. He smiles a dark smile when you nervously try to convince yourself that he won't find you.

He is the nightmare that walks and talks and will always be there when you wake up.

He is as cold as ice.

He is the *Iceman*.

#

It all seemed like a life time ago to Milo now.

Then again, when you've spent half of your life chasing ghosts, you tend to lose track of time in the sense that most of us experience it. That, along with having been a career alcoholic, tends to cloud a person's mind just a tad bit after so many lost years go by like a blur.

And God forbid you keep on drinking excessively, because you could end up being a wino. The only difference between an alcoholic and a wino is that an alcoholic can afford to drink with a roof over his head. He used to be fascinated by winos because he had come so close to becoming one himself.

Luckily for Milo, he didn't up that way – but he came close, and he knew he didn't want to do that; if word got around he wasn't dependable anymore, *he* could end up in the river with his own guts hanging out.

#

His new buddy, Ray, a loan shark, always had work for Milo.

They'd met in a pool hall in Jersey, and had become close friends quickly, Ray being an experienced criminal as well. He knew that Milo had what it took to make it in this business; loyalty.

He knew how to keep his mouth shut, his head down, and his shit wired tight. Ray liked that.

Since the day he'd tested Milo's loyalty – and Milo had passed the test with flying colors – Ray always had someone for Milo to kill.

His job as money collector had quickly become one of not only collecting the money, but "sending a message" to the individual as well. If a guy was late with his payment? Milo would inflict some type of physical pain and injury upon him, just as a reminder *not* to be late again.

If the guy was late over and over again, or didn't pay up at all? Ray would tell Milo to collect what money he could, then kill the guy. If he didn't have *any* money to collect? That wasn't good. Milo would use a pair of pliers to yank out any teeth with gold or silver fillings. If the guy was wearing gold rings? Milo would cut them off, fingers and all.

He always made sure the guy knew *why* he was suffering, too. The message was, *see what happens when you fuck with Ray? Or fuck with me?*

As cold as *ice*.

#

Milo slowly but surely became of the most feared men in the New Jersey crime scene. Word got around fast that if you fucked with Ray or any of his friends or family or business affairs, you would have to deal with the *Iceman*.

Ray would never forget the first time he asked Milo to prove his loyalty. They'd been out driving around in Ray's car when Ray had said, *see that bum over there? On the corner bumming loose change? I want you to go over there and shoot the fucker dead.*

Milo *hated* bums.

Without any argument whatsoever, Milo had signaled Ray's driver to stop the car. He climbed out, walked over to the bum in broad daylight, and placed the barrel of a .38 against the left side of the bum's head, and pulled the trigger. The bum's brains splattered the window behind him. Milo just stood there, smiling. He detached himself from his victims, an attitude that he claims came from having to detach himself from the abuse his drunken father inflicted on him as a boy.

See what you get for being a fucking bum? He thought, grinning. *You get a visit from the Iceman.* Then he just turned around and strolled casually back over to Ray's car and climbed in, grinning. Ray knew then, looking in Milo's cold dark eyes, he had found his new collector-slash-hitman.

His iceman.

#

Milo killed many men for Ray.

But as cold as he was, Milo still had a *code* he lived by.

You *never* hurt women or children.

The first time Ray would ever ask such a thing from Milo would be his *last*. He would ice Ray before he would women or children.

Another code Milo lived by was never, *ever,* run out of money. He had money in three different bank accounts, in a safe deposit box, a post office box, and at home.

Just in case things ever went South on him, he would be prepared. Or if Ray ever got upset with him. Or, his ex wife ever wanted to sue him for extra child support.

He would be *ready.*

But he was hoping that day would never come.

#

In all honesty, Milo was beginning to wonder if Ray was losing his grip on reality.

Lately, Ray was *always* pissed off about one thing or another, losing his temper, and making a fool of himself in public. Milo didn't like that; it tended to attract unwanted attention to him, too.

If Ray ever got angry with Milo, and carried it too far, Milo would have to *ice him,* too.

He wouldn't think twice about doing it, either. He didn't mind having business with "friendly associates," but he didn't have any real friends.

That was another code he lived by; trust *nobody.*

So far, his code had served him well.

He would have to keep a close eye on Ray for now, just to be sure.

#

Milo had heard rumors recently that Ray was using the basement area of his bar, The Gemini Club, as his own private kill room.

Rumors of brutal torture, and the dismemberment of bodies with chainsaws was floating around, and although Milo wasn't really afraid of Ray, he also didn't want to run a chance of being on the recieving end of a chainsaw, either.

So he laid low for the moment, and spent some quality time with his new toy, a crossbow set.

The unpleasant little man at the sporting goods shop had told Milo that the bolts that the crossbow fired could be extremely lethal, and could pierce a deer's skull through and through from one hundred yards away.

But Milo had told the man he hadn't intended to use the crossbow for hunting deer. The man had asked him what he did intend to hunt with it. Milo had just grinned, paid for the crossbow, and walked out.

#

That night, he took a midnight drive into Manhattan again, for some target practice.

He was curious to see what a bolt from a crossbow could do to the skull of a man. He figured that if it could pierce the skull of a deer, it would literally *destroy* the skull of a man.

After driving around for a while, he picked a spot across the street from a bus stop, shut the engine down, rolled down his window, and waited.

He didn't have to wait long.

A tall, thin man dressed in a Polo shirt and dress slacks came strolling toward the bus stop, walking a small dog. Milo hated small dogs. He called them ankle biters.

This dog was a poodle, and he hated poodles as much as he hated queers, which he figured this guy must be, the way he was dressed.

A queer and a poodle.

The perfect target.

Milo placed the crossbow on the edge of the window, took careful aim, and fired, just as the man stopped under a light post to check his wristwatch.

The razor sharp bolt pierced the man's jaw, and came out the other side, pinning his head to the light post. As the man dangled from the post helplessly, screaming in pain and agony, Milo shot the dog next.

He was going to shoot the queer again, but he saw a car coming close by, and not knowing if it was a cop or not, hightailed it out the parking lot in the other direction, and into the darkness of the city.

But he'd be back again.

#

The next day, Ray had a job for Milo.

The job was to collect a large sum of money from a wise guy who had been late with his payment three times.

He'd told Milo, *If the guy says he doesn't have it?*

Milo just grinned and nodded his head and said, *Yeah.*

He had staked out the guy's house for several days, to memorize his daily schedule. He always did that. That way, he'd know when the guy was most likely to be alone, with no witnesses around to give a description of the guy's killer. Using a different weapon each time he killed somebody was just a small part of it. There had to be a period of surviellance and preperation, too.

On the third day he followed the guy to a cheap no-tell-motel where he saw him getting out of his car with a tall blonde hooker. Milo hated hookers almost as much as he hated bums and loudmouths, but he wasn't concerned with her right now.

He sat in his car smoking cigarettes and watching the room from across the street when, after about an hour, the hooker emerged from the room, shoved a stick of gum in her mouth, lit a cigarette, and walked away, toward the nearby tavern. Milo hadn't seen anyone else but her going into the room, so he knew he would be safe, in the cover of night, walking up to the guy's motel door.

He crept up to the door, staying within the shadows, and rapped lightly on the door with his big knuckled hand.

He heard some movement inside, his hearing acute, like a panther, a nocturnal predator. Then, a voice; *Yeah? You forget something, babe?*

He stepped back, and kicked out with his huge

foot and the door burst inward in a haze of broken wood and glass. The door landed on top of the guy inside, pinning him to the floor and knocking the wind out of him. Milo was on top of the door fast, stepping on it hard, hoping he'd crush the guy's ribs.

He said with a big grin, *No, I didn't forget anything. But* you *did. Like your payment to Ray?*

Th guy's eyes flew open with recognition and he begged, *Please, man. Please show some mercy. I got the money, I swear!*

Leaning in close, his eyes filled with hatred and loathing, Milo said, *Sure, I bet you do, asshole.* He pressed down on the door harder with his foot, and heard some of the guy's ribs snap. The guy howled in pain and agony. Milo said, *if you are lying to me about the money, you'll pray for death.*

The guy gasped for breath and said, I *swear! I can get the money! Just let me make a phone call!*

Milo eased up with his foot, letting the guy take a breath. He said, *Okay, asshole, but you better not be lying to me, or you will SUFFER.*

#

The man made the phone call, but the man on the other end hung up on him. He turned to Milo and said, *Please, have mercy, man! I can get the money, it'll just take a little longer.*

Milo said, *How much longer?*

The man said, *Tonight, I swear.*

Milo said, *You best pray you come up with it. As a matter of fact, why don't you pray right now?*

The man said, *Seriously?*

Milo said, *Go ahead and pray, see if God listens to you.*

The man folded his hands and began to pray under his breath. After several minutes, Milo's patience ran dry and he said, *I don't think God is listening to you. I think even God knows a worthless asshole when he sees one.*

The man began sobbing then, down on his knees, begging for mercy. Milo pointed a .38 caliber revolver at his face, and said, *May your God have mercy on your worthless soul.*

Then he pulled the trigger.

#

Afterward, Milo began cleaning up the room, for any blood or fingerprints. He was usually more careful than that, but the guy had really gotten on his nerves, pissed him off, threw him off his game.

He couldn't allow that to happen again.

When he was finished, with the guy's body placed in the bathtub, nude and washed down with bleach, it was time to go.

But not before he took a quick peek around the room for anything the man might have had stashed away.

Under the mattress, he found it; an envelope with almost six-thousand dollars inside, along with a gold ring and wristwatch.

Stupid bastard, he thought. *You died for this? Oh well, it's mine now.*

After placing the envelope in his jacket pocket, Milo left the room, placing the door back on it's frame as best he could, and disappeared into the darkness once again, as always, like a ghost.

The ice man was on a roll tonight.

#

He stopped at phone booth to call Ray. He never used his home phone, it could be traced.

When Ray answered, Milo said, *It's done.*

Ray said, *Did you get my money?*

Milo said, *He didn't have ANY money.*

Ray said, *Then your job ain't done, is it? I want my money, Milo.*

Milo said, *He did have a gold watch and ring, if you want them.*

Ray said, *Why would I want them? It might snag me a lousy three hundred bucks at a pawn shop.*

Milo swallowed his pride and said, *Sorry, boss.*

Ray said, *You're gonna be sorry, asshole, if I don't get my fucking money.*

Then Ray hung up. Milo just stood there staring at the phone, wishing he could choke Ray until his eyeballs popped out, but he knew he had to keep his shit wired tight for now.

#

Milo needed to make more money, and fast.

He drove around the city, chain smoking and racking his brain on how to make more money, but he knew if Ray found out he had any side jobs, he would be dead.

Milo was becoming more and more angry by the

minute.

He needed to vent his frustrations somehow.

He pulled into a parking lot, opened the trunk of his car, and retrieved the crossbow.

Now he could vent his frustrations.

He drove downtown to the poor section of the city, where the hookers and drug addicts and other low lives wandered the streets. Before long, he spotted a tall, thin black man, standing on a street corner, slapping a young woman in the face.

A pimp no doubt, he thought, angrily, and pulled th car over, rolled down his window, and aimed the crossbow at the man's head, and fired.

The bolt struck the man in the left temple, and exited the right side of his head, spraying the woman's face with blood. She screamed as he fell face first on to the sidewalk.

Milo smiled and pulled away, into the bowels of the city again, with a big smile on his face.

#

Milo hadn't been home more than a few minutes when his pocket pager went off. He checked it to see it was Ray's number on the screen.

He called Ray and said, *Yeah?*

Ray said, *Where have you been, Milo?*

Milo said, *I took a drive to clear my head.*

Ray said, *You need to clear it, clean all the shit out of your brain, leaving the body in the motel bathtub.*

Milo played dumb and said, *What the hell are you talking about?*

Ray said, *You know damn well what I'm talking*

about, asshole. Everybody on the street knows you work for me. You might as well have left a note on the door saying Ray was here.

Milo said, *What was I supposed to do? Drag the body out into a busy parking lot?*

Ray said, *I don't give the hairy crack of a rat's ass what you had to do to get it done, you should have just got it DONE. You told me you were a professional.*

Milo said, *I AM a professional.*

Ray said, *Well, Mr professional, you just forfeited half of your fee. You can pick up what's left of it tomorrow.*

Milo said, *That's not fair, I took all the risks.*

Ray said, *Yeah, well, life is a bitch and then you die, remember?*

Ray hung up. Milo said to himself, *Yeah, well, you best remember that too, asshole.*

#

Milo couldn't sleep.

No rest for the wicked, he thought, as his eyes focused on the ceiling above. That thought made him smile.

But he still couldn't sleep.

It was time for another midnight ride.

#

He'd decided to change it up this time, and take his military issue, K-bar knife with him.

It had been a gift from his brother in law, who had served in Vietnam. It was thick, razor sharp, and got the job done every time, and even had sentimental value.

As he drove up and down the dark, filthy streets, he almost wished it would rain, a regular torrential downpour, to wash a lot of the scum from the streets and down the sewer pipes, where they belonged.

Then again, he thought, *I wouldn't have the pleasure of taking one of them out.*

He drove past a dimly lit corner now, the moonlight above barely peeking through the clouds above, when he saw him.

A short, stocky man walking a cat on a leash.

Who in the hell walks a cat on a leash? He thought, not believing his eyes. *Maybe he's a queer. I hate queers as much as I hate cats.*

He pulled over, stopped the car, and shut the engine down, keeping his eyes trained on the man, as he slipped the K-bar knife into his waistband and climbed out of the car, strolling casually over to the corner, as the man stood there looking at his wristwatch.

Milo popped a cigarette in his mouth, approached the man, cracked a big grin, and said, *Hey, fella, you got a light?*

The man smiled and said, *Sure,* and reached into his pants pocket. That's when Milo whipped out the K-bar and shoved the blade into the man's face, right below his chin, the tip of the blade popping out right above the man's nose.

Milo yanked the blade free, as the man fell face forward on to the dirty sidewalk, the cat taking off into the night. Milo thought, *Yeah, you better take off, you little shit.*

Then he went back home and slept like a baby.

#

That is, until his pager went off early the next day.

It was Ray.

Milo didn't feel like driving to a payphone, so he used his land line. He said, *It's a little early, isn't it?*

Ray said, *The early bird catches the worm, remember?*

Milo said, *What's the job?*

Ray said, *Nothing too hard, just a money collection. You OWE me a job, remember?*

Milo said, *Whatever you say.*

Ray said, *It's not what I say, asshole. It's what you owe me.*

Milo said, *I'll be over in a hour.*

#

When Milo arrived at the Gemini Club, Ray was sitting at the bar, already sipping scotch whiskey at nine am in the morning.

Milo knew from past experience that wasn't a good sign. He said, *Having a bad day?*

Ray said, *My day will be a lot better after you get me my fucking money.*

Milo said, *That's what I'm here for.*

Ray took a piece of paper out of his shirt pocket and scooted it across the bar to Milo. He said, *This is the target.*

Milo looked at the paper, memorized it, and wadded it up. He said, *How soon you want it done?*

Ray said, *ASAP.*

Milo said, *I'm on it.*

As Milo walked away, Ray said, *And Milo?*

Milo said, *Yeah?*

Ray said, *Don't fuck this up.*

Milo didn't bother with a reply.

#

The target was a guy named William Roberts, aka "Billy Bob," a loser whose gambling habit had reached epic proportions, and now owed Ray almost eight grand.

Milo found him at a nearby Casino, sitting at the Blackjack table, sweating up a storm as he watched his money get flushed down the crapper yet again. Billy wasn't very good at gambling, but you couldn't tell him that.

But Milo wasn't there to provide financial advice, either.

As he approached Billy Bob from behind, Milo calmly leaned in and whispered in his ear, plain and simple, *Ray wants his money.*

Billy didn't even turn to look at Milo, he just said, *I'm working on that right now.*

Milo glanced at the chips stacked in front of Billy and said, *You stop now, you can pay him back at least five grand. That might save you from at least some physical pain and injury, anyway.*

Again, Billy just said, *I said, I'm working on it. Now fuck off.*

Milo grabbed Billy by the shirt collar and swung him around to face him. Once Billy was forced to look into Milo's eyes, and saw his intimidating physical presence, he grew pale in the face and said, *Can I play just one more hand?*

Milo said, *You play another hand, and lose? It's not just your ass that's in a sling. I think you should stop NOW.*

Billy said, *Just ONE more hand?*

Milo whispered, *How about I BREAK your hands?*

Billy said, glumly, *Okay.* Then he began scooping up his chips and shoving them into his pockets. He said, *Let's go cash them in.*

Then he took off running like the wind, toward the nearest exit door, with Milo right on his tail.

Milo was a large man, but very quick and agile, and he had ahold of Billy within a few seconds, body-slamming him into a parked car, knocking the wind out of him. He flipped him over, stared him in the eyes, and said, *You stupid asshole.*

Begging for his life, Billy said, *Please, Milo. I promise I'll pay it back, but I can't pay it back right now, it's house money.*

Milo said, *What in the hell do you mean, house money?*

Billy said, *A house loan. If I stop now, I won't have enough to make a profit, the money will go straight back to the Casino.*

Milo slammed him against the car again, and said, *You dumb son of a bitch. That's not my problem.*

Billy said, *Let me play some more and I'll split it with you fifty-fifty. I swear.*

Milo thought about it. He was sick of Ray's insults and abuse. Sick of collecting money from dirtbags who said they didn't have any. Sick of getting paid a lousy fee for all of his time and trouble.

He said to Billy, *It will be a seventy-thirty split. Take it or leave it.*

Billy said, *Deal.*

#

Billy's luck had changed.

After several more hours at the Blackjack table, Billy had turned in the loan, with almost four grand left over. After giving Milo his seventy percent, Milo had kept his word, and had allowed Billy to walk away unharmed.

That was his first mistake.

#

That evening, as he sat sipping cold beer and watching TV, his pager went off.

It was Ray.

Milo turned the pager off and went back to watching TV.

About twenty minutes later, there was a knock at the door. Milo ingored it too, until he heard his front door being busted loose from the hinges.

He stomped over to the front door, yanking it open to see Ray standing there, his eyes full of rage and fury. He said, *I was just told Billy boy was walking around, still breathing. That means you must have my money.*

Milo said, *No, I don't. It was house money.*

Ray said, *What the hell is house money?*

Milo said, *You borrow money against the house,*

and pay it before you can make a profit.

Ray said, *That's bullshit. You'd fall for anything, you dumb son of a bitch.*

Doing his best to hold his temper, Milo said, *No, it's not bullshit. I was there.*

Ray said, *Then where is my money?*

Milo said, *I don't have it yet.*

Ray said, *Well, dumbass, Billy boy doesn't have any money, either. My new courier took care of him already. I'd imagine he's floating in the river about now.*

Doing his best to keep his composure, Milo said, *That was MY job.*

Ray said, *And it was your LAST job, for me. Word gets around, too, so I wouldn't waste my time sitting around waiting for any new jobs.*

Milo said, *You son of a bitch.*

Turning to walk away, Ray grinned and said, *You haven't seen anything yet, Milo.*

As Milo watched Ray climb into his Cadillac, he said to himself, *You haven't seen anything yet either, you piece of shit.*

#

Milo didn't stay down for long.

But his worries about money were still there, and growing worse by the minute. He had to find a way to make some money on the side without Ray finding out. He sat racking his brain for ideas, and it suddenly hit him like a bolt of lightning.

His old pool hall buddies, John Hamil, and his good friend Sean, were a couple of guys who he knew he could trust, and were very good at hijacking trucks loaded with TVs, wristwatches, and a lot of other items they could sell to the highest bidder. He'd worked with them before, and made some good money while it lasted.

He went to a nearby payphone and called John. John was thrilled to hear from Milo, knew he could count on him to be the muscle if need be. He said, *Sure, Milo! As a matter of fact, we have a couple of jobs lined up right now, if you're interested.*

Milo said, without hesitation, *When and where?*

#

The job would be a piece of cake; an inside informant named 'Sammy,' gave them the info on a big truck load of expensive TV sets. All Milo, John, and Sean had to do was hijack the truck along it's route, leave the driver tied up and gagged by the side of the road, and drive the truck load of TVs to Sammy's place on the outskirts of town, and stash it in his barn until they found a buyer.

The job went like clockwork, with no complications, and the truck was stashed away as snug as a bug in a rug in Sammy's barn. What they hadn't counted on, though, was it took a week to find a buyer. But the guy was willing to pay top dollar for the goods, so it had been worth the wait.

That is, until they went back to the barn to get the truck, and it wasn't there, and Sammy wasn't anywhere to be found.

Milo was so furious, he vowed to himself if he ever saw Sammy again, he would kill him on sight. But after John and Sean talked him out of it, calmed him down a bit, he agreed to give Sammy the benefit of the doubt until he found out what happened.

They sat in their car and waited for a while, and here came Sammy, walking out of the field behind his house, whistling a happy little tune to himself. Upon seeing the three men climbing out of the car and stomping toward him, his face turned pale and he seemed real nervous. Before he could say a word, Milo grabbed him by the throat and said, *Where in the hell is the fucking truck, Sammy?*

Gasping for breath, Sammy said, *I swear, Milo, I don't know! I was just looking around for it myself! Somebody must have stole it!*

Milo tightened his grip around Sammy's throat and gave him that famous Milo death stare and said, *Uh huh. Somebody just happened along and saw the truck in your barn, and stashed it this close by, where we could find it real easy? You no good motherfucker, I should kill you right now.*

I swear! Sammy repeated, his eyes wide with fear. *I don't KNOW what happened to it!*

Milo threw Sammy to the ground and turned to John and said, *Go get the road flares and rope out of the trunk of my car.*

John shot Milo a funny look and said, *Road flares? What the fuck are you going to do?*

Milo gave John the death stare and said, *Just get the fucking flares.*

In fear of what Milo might do to him and Sean, John obeyed. When he came back with the flares, Milo said, *Now tie him to that tree over there, and take off his shoes and socks.*

Without question, John and Sean did what he said, tying Sammy to the tree with his arms pinned to his sides, and Sean pulled off his work boots and socks. Milo lit up one of the flares, stepped close to Sammy, and said, *Now, you got one more chance to tell me what happened to that truck, or I am going to put you in a world of pain.*

Sammy watched in terror as Milo lowered the burning flare down just close enough to Sammy's right foot to blister the skin. Sammy howled in pain, tears streaming from his eyes. Milo stopped and said, *NOW do you remember what happened to the truck?*

Although Sammy was already in extreme pain and discomfort, he still denied having anything to do with the disappearance of the truck. He said, gasping, *I SWEAR! I don't KNOW!*

Wrong answer, Milo said, and lowered the flare again, this time allowing the flame itself to make contact with the skin. Sammy screamed in pain and agony, trying to squirm free of his bonds, but the rope held tight. Milo pressed the flare directly against the skin, *harder* now, and John and Sean watched in horror as the skin on Sammy's right foot seared away from the heat, exposing the bone.

Milo stopped and said, *Now do you know where the truck is?*

Sammy muttered something but Milo couldn't understand it. Richard said, *I didn't get that. Come again?*

Sammy muttered something unintelligible, so Milo tried to loosen his tongue by pressing the flame directly against his skin again, the flames burning away all the flesh from his toes now, all five bones jutting forth in plain sight. Sammy managed to say, *I swear, I DON'T KNOW.*

John stepped closer, saying, *Milo, nobody could take that kind of pain if he had something to tell you. He doesn't know jack shit.*

Sammy screamed and screamed and squirmed and then mercifully passed out from the pain. Milo stood back, admiring his handiwork, grinning from ear to ear. He said to John, *give him a minute and then wake his ass up.*

After a few moments of glancing at his wristwatch, John stepped up and slapped Sammy in the face hard, bringing him around, but he was still fading in and out of consciousness. Milo grabbed him by the hair and yanked his head up straight, looking him directly in the eyes, and said, *Sammy, do you like your dick?*

Sammy managed to say, *What?!*

Milo said, *I said, do you like your dick? Because if you don't tell me where that truck is, I'm going to burn your dick and balls off.*

Finally, after all of his needless pain and suffering, Sammy screamed, *Okay! Yes! I know where the truck is!*

Milo stopped, dropping the burnt out flare on the ground, shaking his head in disbelief. *Sammy was a tough son of a bitch,* he thought, *but a really stupid son of a bitch, too.*

He looked at Sammy and said, *You mean you knew all this time, and didn't say anything? WHY did you go through all this?*

Sammy said, *I needed the money. I mean, my business is shit, and I got a family to think about, you know? And I got this girl pregnant, she needs an abortion.*

Disgusted with any man who would kill their own unborn baby, Milo said, *Yeah, well, now, she will have to use a coat hanger, won't she?*

John reminded Milo, *So, where is the truck?*

Milo said, *Oh yeah, right. Where is the truck, Sammy?*

Sammy said, *Down the road, there's an old farm. Got a big patch of trees out back of it. Your truck is there, I swear.*

Looking down at Sammy's ruined feet, Milo said, *Oh, don't worry, I believe you this time.* He turned to John and Sean and said, *You boys go get the truck and I will take care of this.*

As they pulled away in Milo's car, he said to Sammy, *Well, was this all worth it, you idiot?*

With tears in his eyes, Sammy said, *No, and you're right, I'm a fuckin' idiot.*

Pulling out one of his guns, Milo said, *That you are, Sammy.* Then he shot him in the forehead.

#

When Milo came home, his phone was ringing.

It was his mother, Anna, calling him to inform him that his younger brother, Joe, had been arrested for the rape and murder of a twelve-year-old girl - and her dog.

Apparently, Joe had lured the girl on to the roof of an apartment building – his good looks and charm too much for her to resist his sweet talking ways – and had paid for it with her life. He had sodomized her, strangled her, and tossed her lifeless body off the roof, her body landing on the concrete below with a sickening, bone-breaking *splat*, in front of tons of witnesses.

He then proceeded to toss her dog off the roof, the poor animal landing on it's legs, breaking all of them on impact. The little dog, even with it's life threatening and painful injuries, managed to crawl over to the girl's body, crying and howling and barking until a neighbor heard the racket and called the police.

Now, knowing he was pedophile as well as a killer, he wanted to *kill* his own brother. He was dead to Milo now, just like his mother and father were, just another disappointing member of a completely dysfunctional and crazy family. In Milo's mind, he was the only *normal* one in the whole bunch.

But still, since Joe was a member of his family, he felt obligated to go see him in jail one time – but it would be the *last* time he would ever see him again.

#

Trenton county jail was a loud, stinking, ugly shit hole.

The perfect place for a low life pedophile like Joe, Milo thought, as he was ushered into the visiting area. The so called visiting area was a tall, solid steel wall with a small window to speak through. It was fine with Milo. The further away from Joe he was the better.

After the guard walked away, Joe was visible on the other side of the glass, looking the worse for wear. Apparently word got around fast about his crimes, and someone had already been at him, beating the shit out of him or even sodomizing him. Which was fine with Milo. He wished they had killed him.

As Milo approached the glass, Joe forced a weak smile and said, *Long time no see, brother. You are looking good.*

Milo forced a smile as well, saying, *Can't say the same for you.*

Joe said, *Oh yeah, well, they are jealous of me in here, you know?*

Feeling sick at his stomach, Milo said, *Jealous? Of a faggot-child molester? I doubt that, brother.*

Infuriated at the remark, Joe said, *Hey! I didn't know how old she was! That little bitch told me she was eighteen!* He sniffled, tears filling his eyes. *And she more or less ASKED for it.*

Milo stepped closer to the glass, infuriated himself now. Wishing he could break through the glass and choke his own brother to death, he said, *You sick fucker. You piece of shit. They said you even killed her dog.*

Joe went crazy then, banging on the glass, bloodying his own knuckles. As the guards ran over to grab him, pulling him away from the glass, Joe screamed, *I am a piece of shit?! You cocksucker! Remember that kid you KILLED with a wooden club, when we were kids, Rich? Huh? Do you? I never told anyone. Maybe I will NOW!*

As the guards dragged Joe away, still screaming at the top of his lungs, Milo actually smiled, knowing his brother wouldn't last long in there. He turned and walked away, feeling like a huge weight had been lifted off his shoulders. He had said goodbye to *all* of his family that day.

#

As he walked out of the prison, he noticed a short, stocky man wearing a white uniform, standing next to an ice cream truck, parked right next to Milo's Buick.

Paying him no mind, Milo began keying his door when the man said, *Hey, big guy.*

Milo said, *Do I know you?*

The man said, *No, but I know you, Milo.*

Milo said, *Who in the hell are you?*

The man said, *The name is Bob. I'm the ice cream man.*

Milo said, *How do you know my name?*

Bob said, *Word gets around on the street, big guy. I heard you might be looking for a job.*

Milo said, *You been talking to a guy named Ray, haven't you?*

Bob said, *That dirtbag? I'd rather slam my nuts in a car door than work for him.*

Milo said, *Then what do you want from me?*

Bob said, *I may have an offer you can't refuse.*

Milo said, *I'm listening.*

Bob said, *You need a job, and I need a partner. We can split any profits fifty-fifty.*

Milo said, *I'm still listening.*

Bob said, *Let's talk about the details somewhere else. The walls around this place have ears.*

#

Milo followed Bob to an old, abandoned warehouse on the edge of the city.

As he exited the Buick, Bob was there, saying, *Follow me, big guy,* and walked up some rickety wooden steps to a large, steel, sliding door with a huge padlock on it. He keyed the door, slid it open, and said, *Come on, big guy,* and walked in first. After Milo was inside, Bob slid the door shut and bolted it from the inside. He said, *I got the perfect set up here. You're gonna love this.*

As they walked through the building, Milo was suddenly overwhelmed by a terrible odor, one he was used to. Bob stopped and said, *Shit! One of the freezers broke down again. Come on.*

Milo followed Bob into a large, walk-in freezer, and lined up on both sides of the room were steel shelves, and the shelves were lined with frozen corpses.

Lying on a steel table nearby was the source of the odor; a body that Bob had forgotten to refreeze. It was partially dismembered, missing the head and hands.

Bob smiled and said, *Oops, false alarm. I forgot to put this one back on ice.*

Milo grinned and said, *An old slaughterhouse, huh? Pretty smart.*

Bob said, *Damn straight it is. It's simple enough, too. I get a job, do the hit, bring them back here, cut them up, freeze them, amd dump them later. That way, the cops have no idea about time or date of death.*

Milo said, *Okay, so how does this deal work out with us?*

Bob said, *That's simple enough, too. We share the hits, share the workload here, and share the profits fifty-fifty, like I said.*

Milo said, *So, you're some kind of "independent contractor" then?*

Bob grinned and said, *Yeah, something like that.*

Milo grinned and said, *Me, too.*

Bob said, *So, do we have a deal?*

Milo said, *Oh yeah, we have a deal.*

Bob said, *Great. Now, help me cut this one up so we can put him back on ice.*

#

Very much like Milo, Bob was also a very proficient killer, and much sought after for his expertise in the art of 'freezing' his victim's remains for an indefinite period of time, therefore assuring a coroner could never determine an exact time of death.

Bob was in reality, a legitimate ice cream vendor, with a fairly profitable business. But being a husband and a father of two children – and in secret a full fledged psychopath – he had to make ends meet somehow. And what better way to make ends meet than doing something he enjoyed, like killing people for money?

He couldn't have picked a better partner than Milo – and vice versa.

The small, out of the way warehouse belonging to Mr Freeze was in a desolate part of the city, far enough away from any really populated areas for him to worry about attracting too much attention to himself.

On their first day working together, when Milo arrived, Bob was smoking a cigarette and sipping a cold beer. He was wearing a long, plastic butcher's apron, stained with blood, and Milo had the strongest feeling Bob hadn't been cutting up poultry.

Milo grinned and said, *So, you been cutting up chickens?*

Bob grinned and said, *Nah, just some stool pidgeons.*

Milo said, *Well let's get to work, then.*

Once inside, Milo was pleasantly surprised with the pristine condition in which Bob kept his workplace. Milo had expected to walk into a dungeon-like atmosphere that reeked of slow rotting death. Instead, his acute sense of smell was overcome by the odor of bleach and other disinfectants, as well as air freshner, all of this having been done since yesterday.

Bob said, glancing around, *Don't let this room fool you, big guy. The main cutting table is in the back. I keep it all seperate from my ice cream coolers. Come on.*

Milo followed Bob through a large steel door into a room that was noticably cooler upon entering, giving Milo the shivers, raising gooseflesh on his arms. He immediately noticed two tall racks of shelves with bodies – or body parts – wrapped in thick plastic. Each bag was adorned with a small paper tag bearing the victim's info; date of death, method of death, etc. He was more impressed than ever now.

Shaking his head in disbelief, Milo said, *Jeez...you really have your shit together, don't you, ice cream man? I have never seen an operation like this.*

His chest swelling with pride, Bob said, *Damn straight, big guy. This operation is top notch. Kept clean, no mess, no evidence.*

Milo was walking along now, between the shelves looking at the bodies through the plastic. He seemed confused, saying, *No stab wounds...no bullet wounds. What is your method of killing them?*

Bob said, *I have no certain MO, that's why I don't get caught. The only MO I have, if you can call it one, is death by poison. No bullet wounds, no leftover slugs fragments, no knife wound impressions can be made. It's quiet – and perfect.*

Milo said, *What kind of poison?*

Bob's favortite method of poisoning his victims was cyanide. It was colorless, odorless, and killed the intended victim quickly, and left behind no evidence other than a possible heart attack. It could be added to food, drinks, or even implemented into an airborne attack – carried in a spray bottle and sprayed directly into the face of the intended victim.

Bob reached into his apron pocket and pulled out a small, glass vile of some white powder. He said, *This is cyanide. Very deadly. This is my baby. No better way to kill than with her.* He kissed the bottle, lovingly, like he would a woman he was sleeping with.

Milo was actually speechless at first, then, *What? You gonna fuck the bottle of cyanide?*

Bob laughed and said, *Really, big guy. This is the BEST way to kill somebody. Put it in their breakfast cereal, spread it on a bologna sandwich, or in a mixed drink. What-the-fuck-ever. It all works the same. And no muss, no fuss, no evidence. It kills quick, too. Two or three minutes, tops. Dead before the ambulance gets there. Looks like a heart attack.*

Milo couldn't help but be impressed, regardless of the fact he thought Bob was a dangerous psychopath. He said, *I want a demonstration.*

#

An up close and personal demonstration is exactly what Milo got.

Merely by coincidence, Bob had a hit lined up for that night, at a local club. The mark was another guy who owed a shitload of cash to the Gambino family, had kept up with flimsy excuses why he hadn't paid up, so he'd more or less signed his own death warrant.

Upon arriving at the club after dark, Milo parking his Buick down the street and away from the bright flash of the neon lights, Bob said, *This is good, big guy. Don't want too far to walk after it's done.*

Shutting off the engine, Milo said, *So, how you going to pull this off in a club full of people?*

Bob said, *Easily, big guy.* He pulled a white handkerchief out of his shirt pocket. *Everyone carries one of these around in there. To wipe the excess coke off their nose before they walk out of the bathroom.*

Impatiently, Milo said, *And?*

And, Bob said, *I just walk by the guy with a spray bottle of cyanide wrapped up in the hanky. When I do a quick pass, I sneeze, like I got a bad cold, at the same time I give him a small squirt directly in the face. He goes down within seconds, and by the time the cops and EMTs get there, we are long gone.*

Cracking a big grin, Milo said, *I want to do this one.*

Glancing around, Bob saw the target walking in, all dressed to kill and his hair slicked back like Al Pacino in *The Godfather.* He motioned to Milo and said, *That's him, the greaseball in the fancy lime green suit. Mr Disco Duck.*

Milo said, *It'll be a pleasure to take him out.*

Bob said, in a whisper, *You want the job? We'll*

split it fifty-fifty. You want the experience anyway, right?

Milo said, *Right.*

Bob low-handed Milo the hanky and the small spray bottle of cyanide. He said, *Just wait until he walks into the bathroom, wait a few seconds, then follow him inside. Pass by him at the sink, fake a sneeze, spray it right in his greaseball face. He'll go down like a sack of fuckin' potatoes.*

Grinning, Milo slipped the goods into his pocket, and kept a close eye on the mark, watching him walking around, strutting his shit, flirting with the ladies. He thought, with a great deal of satisfaction, *Yeah, better enjoy yourself right now, little goombah. You'll be dead in a few minutes.*

It wasn't long before the mark, having just snorted a line of cocaine at the far corner of the bar, stood up and headed toward the men's room. The women he'd been sitting with watched him go, gazing upon him as if he was a famous movie star. Milo looked upon him as a piece of shit he couldn't wait to kill.

Milo waited a few seconds and walked over to the men's room door, pausing to listen for any other voices. Hearing nothing but the sound of the toilet flushing, he walked into the bathroom to see the target standing at the sink, washing his hands. Milo stood at the sink next to him, running a comb through his thinning hairline. He knew he had to move either now or never.

As the target turned to leave, Milo suddenly turned toward him, faked a sneeze and sprayed the deadly poison directly into his eyes. The man immediately began gasping for breath, his eyes wide in pain and terror. His heart rate now three times faster than normal, he began spewing vomit from the corner of his mouth, falling face first on the linoleum floor, breaking his nose on impact.

Milo just stood by the bathroom door, watching him die and relishing every last second of it. Not having time to videotape it for future reference, he wanted to log this wonderful experience into his memory palace forever.

#

Milo, now being experienced in the art of using poison, was now more in demand than ever.

But he had to keep it a secret from Ray. If he ever found out Milo was making money on the side, and not cutting Ray in on the action, Ray would would most likely put a hit out on Milo, and since Milo had seen Ray's private butcher shop-slaughterhouse up close and personal, he didn't relish the idea of Ray finding out about it.

Milo had a good thing going with Mr Freeze now, too, and didn't want to see it end anytime soon. It was the perfect set-up, a partnership made in hell itself. Milo would kill the mark, Bob would provide his private freezer for the storage, and either weeks or months later, they would both share the duty of chopping up the bodies and disposing of them. They shared all profits fifty-fifty, an even split.

But secretly, Milo still had his doubts as to Bob's overall sanity. Yes, Milo knew he was just as cold blooded as they come, but he did have *limits*, depending on the situation, such as his refusal to kill women or children, or kill someone in front of their kids. But Bob, he was a different breed of killer altogether.

He would kill anyone for profit, and even just for the enjoyment of it, the overall thrill of the kill. Men, women, children, animals, he could care less. As he long as he was paid well, or just wanted to kill at the time because it suited him, he did so, without batting an eye. Milo had vowed to himself he would keep an eye on Bob, get used to looking over his shoulder, wished he had eyes in the back of his head.

#

Bob even kept Polaroids of some of his victims. Their hideous portraits were elevated above the stack of skeletal bodies, erected on steel girders high and majestic, looking down on the pathetic waste of what was once human life. To him, they *had* been a waste of life, therefore belonged in his chamber of horrors, their final resting place to be a garbage bag dumped in an undisclosed location, to be devoured by local wildlife, bugs, and maggots. There were all equally worthless to him.

But for now, Milo would do his best to overlook Bob's less than normal character traits, for the sake of the much needed extra income.

Besides, he needed a favor from Bob.

One day, as they sat on the old loading dock sipping cold beer and watching the sun go down, Milo said to Bob, *You know, I could really use a favor.*

Bob said, *Sure, partner. What is it?*

Milo said, *There's this asshole, who works for Ray sometimes. I call him Scooter. Little wiry guy, walks fast, like his ass is on fire. Anyway, I think he's the one Ray has keeping an eye on me.*

Bob said, *Which means he would be keeping an eye on me, too.*

Milo said, *Yeah, I guess you're right.*

Bob said, *Go on, I'm listening.*

Milo said, *Anyway, I was thinking, it would be a damned shame if old Scooter had an "accident."*

Bob grinned and said, *Like what kind of accident?*

Milo said, *Oh, I don't know. How about an "accidental" overdose of cyanide?*

Bob sipped his beer and said, *Sure, big guy. I think I can handle that. How about day after tomorrow?*

Milo said, *Deal.*

#

Two days later, Scooter was on a slab at the warehouse when Milo showed up.

Bob was dressing the body down when Milo walked in, and Milo couldn't help but notice a huge gash across Scooter's throat, from ear to ear. He said, *I thought you were going to use cyanide.*

Bob said, *I was, but changed my mind at the last minute. I figured since you seemed to dislike him so much, I would make him suffer a little. Any objections?*

Milo said, *No, none at all.* But he didn't mean it. It did worry him. He knew then that he and Bob would have to part ways.

Which meant Bob would have to die, too.

#

Milo had used Bob's own special brand of murder to kill him.

Two days later, he had invited Bob to a special little "picnic" in the nearby park, in which Milo had made special sandwiches – Bob's laced with cyanide – to celebrate their partnership.

Bob hadn't even washed the first bite down with his beer when he began to choke to death, It hadn't taken long. But as he died, he looked Milo in the eyes – an accusatory look, one of extreme betrayal – and then he died.

As Milo stood up from the picnic table, he'd said, *It was nothing personal, Bob. Just business, remember?*

For Milo, it *was* just that; only business – the business of cold blooded murder.

#

The very next day, Milo got a call from Ray.

He drove to the nearest phone booth and called Ray, and said, in a pleasant tone, *Long time no hear. What's up boss?*

Ray said, *Murder is what's up. Back stabbing and lying is what's up.*

Feigning ignorance, Milo said, *Come again?*

Ray said, *Don't play dumb with me, asshole. You know what I'm talking about.*

Milo said, *No, I don't.*

Ray said, *Yeah, I bet you don't. You remember Scotty, don't you? The guy I heard you refer to as Scooter?*

Milo said, *Vaguely, yes. What about him?*

Ray said, *Well, yesterday, I receive this cute little*

gift box in the mail. Inside is Scotty's left ring finger, still adorned with a nice tiger's eye ring I bought him for Christmas last year.

Milo said, *Damn, boss. I'm sorry.*

Ray said, *Yeah, I bet you are.*

Milo said, *Meaning?*

Ray said, *Meaning, each and every time you and me lose touch temporarily, something bad happens to one of my crew. I'm going to give you one more chance to prove yourself, but if you fuck it up, I'll be coming after you, and your whole fucking family. I'll cut out your wife's eyes, and make you watch. Then I'll make your kids die real SLOW.*

Milo knew Ray was serious. He said, *Okay, Ray. I understand.*

Ray said, *You better, asshole, and be here at the Gemini Club first thing in the morning.*

Then Ray hung up. Milo did too, thinking, *Great. Now I will have to kill Ray, too.*

#

Ray was always calling him, day and night, needing him to kill someone.

One night he would be using road flares to burn off a man's balls, the next night using a knife to slice layers of skin off another victim, another night using his trusty old .22 pistol to ventilate someone's head.

Jobs and jobs and more jobs came his way, so many at one point, the value of human life had no meaning at all to him any more, and not that it had much to begin with.

But, he was, after all, the Iceman.

#

Unknown to Ray, once again, Milo had even started a burglary ring with four other men he thought he could trust, for extra income. He was spiralling out of control. Killing, drinking, gambling, stealing, and pornography.

The four men he entrusted to run his B&E {breaking and entering} operation, Al Rinke, Gary Smith, Danny Deppner, and Percy House, none of which were too smart, were still very trustworthy otherwise, so Milo tended to overlook their lack of education.

The operation was simple enough; case the houses ahead of time, break into homes all over New Jersey, and carry out anything of monetary value, including jewels and even cars stolen from their victim's garage. Then Milo would let an old friend, Phil Solimene, sell the goods, and then split the profits with the gang members.

Meanwhile, Milo was doing what he did best; collecting or killing for Ray.

#

Then one night, as he sat at his apartment eating a deli sandwich and watching TV {he sure missed Barbara's cooking} he thought, *Now that I'm making BIG money, I could set some back for my girl's college fund.*

He bet Barbara would like to hear that, too.

He picked up his land line phone and dialed his old number. She answered on the fifth ring, sounding out of breath. *Hello?*

He said, *How's it going babe?*

She said, in a sarcastic tone, *How do you think it's going?*

Trying to ignore her sarcasm, he said, *How are the girls doing?*

She said, *How do you THINK they're doing?*

He said, *I didn't call to argue, Barbara.*

She said, *Then why did you call?*

He said, *I'm thinking about setting up a college fund for the girls. I thought you would be happy about it.*

She said, *Oh no, Milo. I don't want your dirty money.*

He said, *Dirty money?*

She said, *YES, your DIRTY money. The money you made from being a CRIMINAL.*

He said, *I don't know what you're talking about.*

She said, *Yes you do, Milo. You're just too much of a heartless criminal and coward to admit the truth.*

She hung up. He just sat there for a few moments, staring at the reciever, as though it was a portal into another dimension, and someone had slammed the door shut, trapping him there.

Then he exploded, his temper getting the best of im again, as it always did.

Just like the night he had slapped his wife so hard, her orbital socket had been fractured. Or the time he'd come home intoxicated again, and had proceeded to turn the living room into a disaster area with his bare hands.

Those were the *only* memories he'd be left with for now.

After he'd punched the kitchen cabinets into tiny pieces of bloody timber, he'd sat down at the table, sipping bourbon, chain smoking, and trying his best to gain his composure back.

Before someone got hurt.

Before an innocent stranger paid the price for his anger and frustration.

A few minutes later, he grabbed his crossbow, and went out for a midnight ride.

#

He went on a regular killing *spree*.

He had begun to become bored with 'regular' ways of killing people – guns or knives – and had decided to spice it up a little bit, using his bare hands to beat them and choke them, as well as other horrifying methods of murder.

He would use a crowbar to beat them, breaking their kneecaps and arms. He would use a fifteen inch screwdriver to stab them in the spine, leaving them paralyzed but still alive to endure even more torture. Sometimes he would take mercy upon them and just smash their skull in with a large hammer – but not very often.

After he was finished with them, he would chop them up, place their body parts in fifty-five gallon drums, seal the top, cut holes in the sides so they would sink, then dumped them in the nearby Hudson River, for the crabs and other sea life to devour the rest of the remains.

In Milo's opinion, life was good.

But as usual, life would throw him another curve ball, each new one more daunting than the last one.

#

Danny Deppner, one of Milo's B&E crew, had been arrested and charged with possession of stolen property.

Upon finding out about Danny's arrest, Milo had been concerned at first, but after thinking it over, had decided that he was the *Iceman*, so who could touch him? And besides, Danny was trustworthy, right? He knew better than to squeal on Milo, in fear of of his wrath. He knew enough about Milo to double cross him in any way.

What Milo hadn't counted on, though, was Danny's so called wife, Bobbie, an alcoholic and drug addict – and now pregnant by Danny's co-worker, Percy House – opening her big mouth about their recent activities.

After Danny's arrest, she had flipped out, going straight to a detective working the B&E case, Patrick Kane, and had proceeded to spill the beans.

As far as Milo was concerned, Bobbie had to *die*.

#

But, first things first.

First, he had to bond Danny out of jail, assemble the whole crew somewhere private, and see if anyone needed to die along with her.

#

Danny's bond was twenty-thousand dollars, which had Milo pissed off already.

As soon as he had bailed him out, they had immediately driven to a nearby motel room Milo had rented, where the rest of the gang was waiting for them.

After they were all gathered in one room, Milo had stood before them, smoking a cigarette and saying to Danny, *So, Danny boy. I guess you already know why we're all here.*

Danny said, *Wait now, big guy. You know me, and know I would never tell the boys in blue anything about our operation.*

Milo said, *I want you to look me in the eyes, and tell me you'd never fuck me over.*

Danny said, nervously, *I would NEVER fuck you over, Milo.*

Milo looked at Gary, Al, and Percy, and said, *What about you guys? Would you ever fuck me over?*

They all shook their heads NO, and Percy said, *You know me, Milo. You know all of us. There's no way we would do that shit.*

Milo thought, *Yeah, right, Percy. You'd never screw anyone over. Just like you're not screwing Danny over by screwing his wife.*

Milo said, *It's okay, I believe you. Now, why don't we celebrate? I'll go grab some take out burgers and beer, and we'll have us a little party?*

Danny said, *That's cool with me. That jail food tastes like shit.*

\#

After Milo had returned with the burgers – the ones laced with cyanide – and he had watched the crew die slow, excruicating deaths, Milo had dragged all of the bodies into the bathroom, stacked the bodies in the shower, closed the bathroom door, and left, knowing he had only one loose end left to take care of.

Bobbie Deppner.

#

On the way over to the Deppner home, Milo could just hear Bobbie's voice in his head, singing like a canary to the cops.

He's a stone cold killer, he is! He ENJOYS killing people. He's fucking crazy!

He knew she would talk.

He didn't believe in killing women, but in Bobbie Deppner's case, he was willing to make an exception. He knew her kids would be better off without her too, and being adopted by a family that might treat them right, give them a decent life.

He would be doing the world a favor.

So he did.

#

It hadn't taken long.

He had been lucky enough to catch her as she exited the shower, caught her off guard.

She didn't even have time to scream, before he had ahold of her, by the throat, his large, beefy fingers crushing her windpipe.

Afterward, he placed her body in the trunk of his Buick, drove to the river, and dumped her body where it would be found, so word on the street would be, *You screw with the Iceman, here's what happens.*

Later, at home, he sipped beer, ate some lefteover chili, and slept like a baby.

#

To make matters worse for Milo, though, Ray's fool-proof life of crime was beginning to unravel as well, which Milo knew, of course, would leave him wide open for even more trouble, once Ray began singing like a canary to the cops to save his own ass.

Milo now had an unhappy, suspicious ex-wife, a promiscuous daughter, another daughter who was in total fear of her own father, and was watching his whole life he'd worked so hard for coming apart before his very eyes. His overall demeanor had taken a turn for the worse as well, making him even more unpredictable and violent than ever before.

But he still kept on killing.

It was in his blood, his DNA. It was like he was born with a killer gene in his body, one that had instilled in him the constant urge to kill, the craving for blood and death. If he wasn't killing someone, making them suffer, it was like a very vital part of him was missing.

Milo had made the decision that Ray had to die.

The last time Milo had seen Ray in person, he could tell he was losing control, lacking cohesion. Ray's general appearance had told the whole story. Wrinkled clothing, hair uncombed, dark circles under his eyes, liquor on his breath. His eyes were wild, darting around the room whenever he spoke, as if he were a fox trapped in a cul-de-sac, expecting a pack of hounds to appear at any moment, ready to tear him apart.

Milo would be that hound, and would most definitely tear Ray apart.

#

But, as usual, first things first.

First, he would have to make sure there would be nobody or nothing left behind to connect Milo to any of his past crimes, so there would be no or at least very little evidence to use against him in a court of law.

Should I start with Ray? He thought. *Or save him for later?*

Milo needed to start making these important decisions - and *fast*.

He decided to begin with Ray.

#

Milo took a drive to the nearest payphone, and called Ray at home.

There was no answer.

He called the Gemini Club, and Ray answered on the fifth ring. *Yeah, Milo?*

Milo said, *Haven't heard from you lately. Is there a problem?*

Ray said, *Oh yeah, there's a problem. I heard from a reliable source the Feds are on my tail.*

Milo said, *So, no jobs for me, then?*

Ray said, *Clean out your fucking ears, Milo. I said, the Feds are watching me. I'm in the middle of cleaning up the basement as we speak.*

Milo remembered all too well what went on in the basement of the Gemini Club. He said, *Need any help?*

Ray said, *Are you serious?*

Milo said, *Is it a paying job?*

Ray said, *I'll pay you what I can AFFORD to pay you, dumbass. Take it or leave it.*

Milo said, *I'll be there in an hour.*

#

When Milo walked down the steps to the basement, he was almost overwhelmed by the odor of bleach and other disinfectants.

The so called "cutting room" was disgusting, even for Milo's tastes. Blood stains on the walls, tiny pieces of flesh and bone littered the floor. He saw a tooth and an eyeball in one corner.

Milo said, *Damn. This place reeks.*

Ray said, *No shit, genius. Just pick up a mop and get busy.*

Milo said, *You don't need a mop, you need a fucking bulldozer.*

Ray said, *Just get busy smartass.*

#

It took almost four hours, but they had the cutting room as clean as it was going to be.

Afterward, as Milo and Ray sat at the bar, sipping beer and listening to the radio, Milo said, *So, the Feds, huh?*

Ray said, *Yeah. They're watching me like a hawk. I can't make any money right now, either, unless it's selling apples on the street corner. Every penny has to be legitimate for now.*

Milo said, *So, I guess I'm unemployed after today, huh?*

Ray said, *Sorry, Milo. For now, you're going to have to be retired.*

Milo said, *That's okay, Ray, I understand. And I hope you understand, too.*

Ray said, *Come again?*

That's when Milo *snapped*, pulling out the .38 and firing five shots into Ray's body, three bullets in his chest, one in his face, and one in the forehead, killing him instantly. But that wasn't good enough.

He then beat the dead man with the butt of his revolver, crushing the bones in his face to a bloody pulp, cursing him the whole time, as if Ray could still hear him.

Afterwards, Milo tossed Ray into the trunk of his own car and left him there to be found, wanting *everyone* to know what happened when you fucked with the Iceman.

One down, many more to go.

#

He was so used to causing the deaths of others, he didn't even realize he was digging his *own* grave.

Tonight, he had become bored laying low and watching TV, and had decided to take one of his midnight rides.

Milo drove around in his Buick, watching people walking down the street, some of them on their way home, some of them on their way to the local taverns, and some on their way to oblivion, as far as he was concerned.

He hadn't been driving around long when he spotted a man hitch-hiking, his thumb out by the side of the road. Milo stopped, rolled down his window, and asked the man where he was going. The man said something – which Milo paid no attention to, he was raising the crossbow up to the edge of the window – and before the man could finish a sentence, Milo fired the weapon, the six-inch steel bolt piercing his skull, just above his right eye, and into his brain, killing him instantly.

Milo was now becoming even more explosive and homicidal, venting his frustrations on innocent victims all over again.

Only a few minutes later, he spotted his second victim, a tall, skinny man with tattered clothing and dirty, grimy fingers, no doubt just a derelict out digging in dumpsters. Milo hated the homeless, and hated how pushy they could become when they wanted a handout. He considered them a worthless waste of life and breath, and this one, as far as he was concerned, had to die. Nobody would care anyway. He was doing the world a favor.

He pulled up along side of the man, as he stopped to lean against a light pole to catch his breath, and fired the weapon directly at the man's chest. The arrow went in close to the man's heart and exited out the back side just between his shoulder blades, pinning him to the pole.

He just hung there, weaving back and forth like a drunken puppet, blood oozing from his mouth until he died. Milo sat watching him die, enjoying it, fascinated by how quickly and efficiently the crossbow could kill someone.

Milo then drove on into the darkness, cruising the streets for more victims, until the early light of dawn came up over the horizon. By the time he'd parked his Buick in the driveway, he'd killed six people with the crossbow, and made a mental note to buy more arrow bolts in the morning.

So little time, so many people to kill.

#

Including Ray's two favorite associates, Henry Borelli and Joe "Dracula" Bugliami, the latter of which was Ray's own cousin.

Milo knew he would be the first and only suspect in their eyes; they had been sitting in the parking lot of the Gemini Club the day Milo came to help Ray clean up the cutting room.

By now, they'd found Ray's body, and would out for blood.

Milo's blood.

#

He rented a motel room in East Jersey, under and assumed name, and waited it out – but not for long.

He knew Henry and Joe were like blood hounds if they were on someone's trail, so he would have to lay low, at least for now. Then, when the time was right, he would strike.

So for now, he would sit in his room, watch TV, drink beer, and relax.

But not for long.

After several days, he got the old *urge* again, and couldn't sit still any longer.

He called an old friend, Vito Spinelli, who was an

arch enemy of Ray and his goons, and asked him if he had any jobs currently open.

To Milo's delight, he was offered a job going after a man named John Spasudo, a gambling addict and sexual deviant who was in deep with some Italian mobsters for over one-hundred-thousand dollars. It would be a big payday for the big guy, and he couldn't turn it down, regardless of his hectic schedule – and his concern about Henry and Joe.

On the phone, he asked Vito, *So, what's the split going to be?*

Vito said, *Sixty -forty, as always.*

Milo said, *Fair enough. When and where?*

Vito said, *Drop by my place later today, and I'll fill you in on the details.*

Milo said, *Sounds good, talk to you later.*

After he hung up, Milo smiled, laid back on the bed, and day dreamed on how he was going to spend the forty-thousand dollars.

#

As it turned out, his happiness was short lived.

A real charmer and a smooth talker, Spasudo had made the mistake of thinking he'd be able to charm the pants off Milo, but he'd heard the same old bullshit excuses too many times in the past to listen for long. He politely but firmly informed Spasudo he would have to get nasty about it if he didn't come up with the money right away, and to Milo's surprise, Spasudo readily agreed, and promised to have the full balance he owed within a few days.

Milo had called Vito with the news, and Vito had

said, *Big guy, I know we've been amigos for a long time, but, if you don't get that money by tomorrow night, our agreement will be dissolved.*

Milo had said, *Are you serious?*

Vito had said, *As a heart attack. By tomorrow night, Milo. End of discussion.*

Then Vito hung up on Milo, and wouldn't answer the phone when Milo called back. Milo just laid back on the bed again, lit a cigarette, and began wondering if he'd have to kill Vito, too.

Milo rarely made any real friends, and when he did, they didn't seem to last very long.

#

The next day, Milo dropped by Spasudo's place, early, and staked it out from across the street.

He hadn't been there long when Spasudo came walking out, carrying a big suitcase, tossing it in the back seat of his ancient Volvo, then clmbing into the driver's seat to pull out of his driveway.

Milo started his engine, and floored the gas pedal, pulling right up behind Spasudo's car, blocking him off. He was out of the Buick and standing next to the driver's side window within seconds, the .38 in his hand.

He said, *Going somewhere, John? Maybe the Bahamas?*

Nervously, Spasudo smiled and said, *Just going to the diner for some breakfast, want to come along?*

Milo pointed the gun barrel right at Spasudo's face, and said, *I just want my fucking money.*

Spasudo said, *Like I said, Milo, might be a couple of days.*

Milo said, *Not good enough. I want the money now, or I'll ventilate your head.*

Spasudo said, *Please, Milo, just one more day?*

Milo said, *NOW, John. Give me the fucking money, or I'll put a bullet in your eyeball.*

Spasudo said, *Please, Milo, have some pity.*

Milo almost put a bullet in his eye, but suddenly thought the better of it. He had a much better idea.

He said, *Why don't we take a ride, John?*

Spasudo said, nervously, *A ride?*

Milo said, *Yeah, I want you to see my pets.*

Spasudo said, *Pets? You mean like a dog?*

Milo said, *No, not like a dog or a cat. These are very special pets.*

Spasudo said, *I'd rather go to the diner.*

Milo placed the barrel of the .38 against Spasudo's head, and said, *Out of the car now, or I will shoot you, John.*

Spasudo took a deep breath, and climbed out of the Volvo, with his hands half raised in submission. Milo said, *Now, climb into the front seat of the Buick, and put your seatbelt on.*

As Spasudo did what he was told, Milo grabbed the suitcase out of the back seat of the Volvo, and carried it over to the Buick, placing it in the trunk. He unzipped it and looked inside to see stacks of cash, and estimated there was at least eighty grand in there. He thought, *You weasly little son of a bitch.*

He zipped the suitcase back up, closed the trunk, and climbed into the driver's seat of the Buick, and said, *Where is the rest of it, John?*

Spasudo said, *Like I said, I need more time.*

Starting the engine, Milo said, *You just ran out of*

time, John.

#

Milo had seen a horror film in which a man was tied to a tree and cut up to bleed – non-fatal wounds at first – just enough blood flow to attract the army of rats that were set loose upon him, eating him alive – slowly and painfully picking the flesh from his bones.

He knew there were plenty of hungry rats near the county landfill, so he took Spasudo there, to introduce him to his *pets.*

As they pulled up behind the county landfill office, their presence blocked by a large row of dead trees, Milo parked and shut the engine down, and said, *Get out, John.*

Spasudo said, *Please, Milo. Just give me until tomorrow. I swear I'll have the money.*

Milo pointed the .38 at him, and said, *OUT, John. Get out of the car now.*

Spasudo obeyed, climbing out of the Buick slowly, unsteady on his feet. He leaned up against the car and said, *Well, get on with it, you heartless son of a bitch.*

Milo grinned and said, *I can be, yes. Now, step over there, to that old dead tree next to the shack.*

Spasudo obeyed him once again, walking slowly toward an old wooden shack, the door hanging loose from the hinges, aged with time and rust and rot.

Then he saw the old, dried up blood stains right inside the doorway. *He said, So, this is where it ends, huh? Next to the city dump in some shithole shack over a lousy twenty grand?*

Pointing the .38 at Spasudo's head, Milo said, *It didn't have to be this way, John. Now, go on, into the shack.*

Spasudo slowly walked into the shack to see an old wooden chair, stained with blood, and small pieces of bone – and a human skull – lying on the floor nearby. The skull had small teeth marks on it.

Spasudo said, Please, Milo! *I swear I will pay Ray off and he will never see me again! I swear! I will move to fuckin' China!*

Milo said, *Go ahead and have a seat, John. Have a seat and meet my pets.*

Spasudo got down on his knees, and said, *PLEASE, Milo! You can't do this!*

Milo said, *Sit down, or I'll break your legs.*

Spasudo reluctantly sat down on the chair, and at the same time, Milo shot him in both kneecaps. Spasudo cried out in pain and agony, as Milo held him upright in the chair, handcuffing him to it, so he wouldn't be able to move.

As Spasudo sat screaming, Milo said, *That's it, John. Scream and cry and whine like a pussy, let my pets know you're HERE.*

Then Milo walked away, leaving Spasudo behind, inside the death shack, to let his *pets* take care of the rest.

He could still hear Spasudo screaming a block away, as blood pumped in small rhythmic spurts from the open wounds with each beat of his terrified heart, as the rats began gnawing at his kneecaps.

#

By the time Milo returned, Spasudo's lower body was mostly bloody bone, and he had long since passed out from the pain and torture of having his skin and flesh chewed away by the vile little beasts.

His job was done and as usual, there would be no evidence left of the crime, nothing to tie it to Milo.

Then he climbed back in the Buick to drive over to Vito's place with the money – but on the way there, he had a change of heart.

Milo figured, after all of the shit he'd been through obtaining the money, he was entitled to a bigger cut.

Eighty thousand divided by two is bullshit.

But...eighty thousand divided by *zero*, means Milo is a rich man again.

He stopped at a phone booth and called Vito.

Vito answered on the first ring, and he sounded very impatient. *Where is my money, Milo?*

Milo said, *He didn't have it.*

Vito said, *That's bullshit.*

Milo said, *Well, I searched his house and car and there was nothing.*

Vito said, *Bullshit, Milo. He always has money. You wouldn't be trying to screw me, would you?*

Milo said, *You know me better than that.*

Vito said, *I thought I did. Word on the street has it that you took out Ray. He was associated with the Gambino family. That means you're a target. Which also means you need all the money you can get right now.*

Milo said, *Like I told you, Vito, he did NOT have any money.*

Vito said, *Where is he now? Spasudo?*

Milo said, *He's rat food. Don't worry about him.*

Vito said, *Now, that I can believe. You don't want any witnesses left behind to show that YOU are a rat.*

Milo said, *Watch your mouth, Vito. Just watch your fucking mouth.*

Vito said, *Or what? You gonna come after me? That's a laugh. Oh, and best watch your back, grow a pair of eyeballs in your asshole, because I know for a fact that Henry Borelli and Dracula Joe are hot on your trail.*

Milo said, *I ain't worried about those punks. You seem to forget who you're talking to here.*

Vito said, *Oh, I know who I'm talking to, I'm talking to a DEAD man.*

Vito hung up. Milo did too, slamming the phone reciever down so hard in the cradle it broke into two pieces.

Fuck you, Vito, he said to himself. *Fuck you and our punk friends.*

Then he climbed into the Buick and headed back to the motel, post haste.

#

Whne he got back to the motel, he could see an older model Cadillac parked outside, and his motel room door was hanging wide open.

He slammed on the brakes, put the car in reverse, and backed up beind a large dumpster. As he sat watching the doorway, he could see Henry and Joe walking out now, both of them looking left to right, as if searching the parking lot for someone.

For *him.*

Then they walked back inside, no doubt to make

themselves comfy, at his expense, and wait a little longer to see if he came back.

He slowly backed the Buick out from behind the dumpster, and pulled back out on to the main highway, not sure where he was going until he got there.

#

Despite Milo's mild concern over Henry and Joe watching him like a hawk, he continued to pursue his criminal enterprises full throttle.

But while Milo's retirement fund was getting bigger and bigger by the day, so were his chances of getting nailed by the Gambino family.

He had been acting as a freelance killer across the river in Manhattan, but he knew that eventually, word would spread across the river too, about the price on his head, and he'd be a target there too.

But, he had the money now he could use to disappear forever. Then again, his kids were here. It was a hard choice to know what to do.

In the end, he had decided to stay in an area he was used to, and keep his fingers crossed.

That was his first mistake.

#

Renting another motel room in a different part of the city, Milo had felt safe for the time being – that is, until the morning he walked out of his motel room door, to see Henry and Joe waiting for him right outside.

He had just climbed out of the shower, had dressed in his casual clothes – jeans, boots, a short sleeved shirt – and had lit a cigarette and was going to watch the sunrise, just like he and Barbara used to do.

At one time, the sunrise in Jersey were something they'd grown to love. The way everything turned to a blinding gold and shined as if it were the only place on the earth. As if the sunrise was meant for them alone.

And it was. Each morning as Milo stood with his back against the door frame, watching the sun come up, he forgot – at least for the time being – there had ever been a place where the sky always seemed dull and dark, and now the scent of early morning dew was his favorite perfume, as it seemed to emanate from Barbara's glowing skin.

But that was long ago and far away, now.

As he opened the door, there was Joe and Henry, sitting on the hood of his Buick, the both of them grinning like a Cheshire cat.

Theyd didn't know it, but Milo had his .38 stuffed into the back of his waistband.

Joe said, *Long time no see, Milo. You don't look so good.*

Henry chimed in and said, *Yeah, he looks like he is worried about something.*

Staring them down, *Milo said, I ain't worried about anything. YOU should be the ones worried.*

Reaching into the pocket of his jacket, Henry pulled out a .25 automatic equipped with a silencer. He said, *I don't think so, big guy.*

Joe pulled a large hunting knife from his waistband, and said, *I think we should go back in the room, have a little party.*

Henry said, *Yeah, that's a good idea.*

Milo said, *Listen, guys. I'll give you one chance to*

leave. It doesn't have to end like this.

Henry grinned and said, *Yes, it does, big guy. You shouldn't have killed Ray.*

Milo said, *Ray was an asshole, and you should know that. You both kissed his ass enough.*

Joe said, *I ain't kissed anybody's ass. Who the hell do you think you're talking to?*

I think I'm talking to a piece of shit, Milo said, pulling his .38 from his waistband. He shot both of them in the face, and they slid off the hood of the Buick and hit the concrete.

Milo quickly grabbed both of the bodies and dragged them inside the room, and dumped them on the bed. Henry was still alive, trying to speak, but was choking on his own blood.

Milo said, *What was that? I can't hear you, asshole.*

Henry spat a mouthful of blood on the bed sheet, and said, *I'll see you in hell, Milo.*

Milo said, *Yeah, and I'll shoot you there, too.*

Then he shot him again.

#

After packing the trunk of the Buick, Milo left the motel behind, knowing now that he would have to find a another car, too; his Buick stood out like a sore thumb in Jersey.

But *buying* a new car would leave a paper trail.

He would have to *steal* a new car – and this time, he wanted a Cadillac.

#

After dark, downtown, he'd found a decent looking Cadillac – with the keys inside, no less - parked outside a night club, some strip joint called the Titty Twister.

He had parked the Buick about a block away, walked back to the club, swapped out the plates, and climbed in, turning on the radio and lighting a cigarette and thinking, *Hey...this isn't so bad. Not too bad at all.*

Then, blaring the radio and rolling down his window, he sped off into the night, into the bowels of the city once again, for some target practice.

He *never* got tired of target practice.

#

Once he'd rented a new motel room – this one with free HBO and a vibrating bed – he'd been searching through his big duffle bag for his crossbow when someone had knocked on the door.

Grabbing the .38 and creeping quietly over to the door, looking through the little peephole, he saw one of the house maids standing there, holding a newspaper.

He slipped the .38 into the back of his waistband, and opened the door, and said, *Yes, may I help you?*

She showed him the front page of the newspaper and said, *I'm going around to each room and letting our guests know that they should stay in and be careful tonight. There's some crazy man going around killing folks!*

Milo glanced at the newspaper to see the front page read:

Is There A Serial Killer Walking Our Streets?!

Milo didn't have to read the article to know who it was referring to; over the last few weeks, he'd left behind a trail of dead bodies a mile long.

He smiled and said, *Oh my. That's terrible. I'll be sure to be careful, ma'am. Thank you so much.*

Have a good night, she said, with a big smile, and toddled off to the next room to knock on the door. Milo closed his door, and, after making sure it was locked up tight, laid down on the bed to watch HBO.

No target practice tonight.

#

As the days wore on, Milo's urge grew stronger, and his resistance weaker.

Sitting at the small table and playing solitaire or watching HBO wasn't so satisfying any more. He needed to get some exercise. Something to calm his urges and keep his sanity intact before he went off the rails.

He opened another beer, and sipped slowly, knowing he wouldn't have another one untl the liquor store made a delivery around noon. Just like his food supply wouldn't be replenished until the grocery store made another delivery later that afternoon.

He felt like a *prisoner,* and he didn't like that.

He had dealt with enough of that as a child; love malice, and malice love – and nobody to help him escape his prison.

He grabbed a pad of paper and an ink pen, sat

back down at the table, and began writing.

Jotting down whatever came to mind, in order to *clear* his mind.

Or his soul.

A serial killer.

That's what I am in every sense of the word.

If I thought someone should die, they would.

It was my way of life, it would never be changed. I wouldn't let it change.

It would be painless and easy for them.

For me? I'd have to live with it.

That wasn't a big deal.

The big deal was the cleaning up.

It was a pain in my ass.

A huge pain in my ass.

A pain I had to deal with.

The only joy I ever get out of them is killing them.

Hearing their neck snap, hearing their bones crunch, watch their blood flow and hearing their heart stop.

It welcomes me.

It makes me feel like I could survive a few decades, and still keep half of my sanity.

It is the epitome of my existence.

It meant nothing to me.

I was a serial killer.

This is my life.

I was BORN to kill.

He stopped writing, sat back and looked over what he'd written.

He didn't feel any better.

He still had that *urge*.

He knew now that the urge wouldn't go away until he took a midnight drive.

He spent the next few hours trying to sleep, but sleep wouldn't come to him.

#

Around ten PM, after a late dinner of takeout tacos and beer, he had decided to take a walk.

He was going to drive the Cadillac, but had decided to take a walk instead. He hadn't taken a stroll among the sheep for a while, and wanted this next experience to be *up close and personal.*

See the lights in their eyes fade out.

He walked into the nearby park, waiting in the shadows.

#

The man hung there naked in the shadows a few feet away, tied to a tree. His shoulders shaking as he caught his breath. Milo could literally sense the fear rolling off of him. It was simply wonderful.

The man said, *Please sir, I won't tell anyone I promise. Just don't hurt me anymore!* he pleaded, but Milo had other plans for him. If he thought the bloody nose and black eye and the superficial knife wounds were bad, he hadn't seen anything yet.

The forest looming around him made it worse.

The trees crushed darkly around him. His fear escalating into pure panic mode. He knew that there was no way out. The beast had captured his prey. He cried out as his ankle twisted. There was no hope for him now. He did the only thing he could think to do.

He begged again.

Said he'd do ANYTHING if Milo stopped hurting him.

Milo said, *I know you will do anything I want you to, that's the fun part.* He brandished the blood stained knife and the young man's eyes filled with tears. *But you know what the most fun part of it is?*

The young man shook his head no, stalling for time. Time of which he had none left of within the next few moments.

I know you are scared, terrified. Of course, let me help you. Milo said. His voice coming out in a purr. *Let me end your pain.*

So he did.

As he stood back watching the young man's carotid artery spurting blood three feet into the air, Milo finally felt as though he could go back to his motel room and get a good night's sleep.

#

For the first time in days, he slept like a baby.

He awoke around three am, sipped a beer, smoked a couple of cigarettes, then tried going back to sleep.

But sleep wouldn't come to him this time.

He needed to take another walk.

#

It was the dead of night, the moon was shining through the hazy clouds making it possible to see a few yards ahead of himself, perfect hunting weather, he thought to himself. He started as he normally does, sharpening his knife and taking his position close to the nearby overpass.

He'd seen many a hitchhiker here recently.

He chose his spot carefully. He was starting to get quite a name around in Jersey, the *devil*, they are calling him, how pathetic they were, almost made him think that his killings might have purpose, of course they didn't, he just killed for the fun of it. He liked hearing the screams of the tortured victims as they died writhing in pain from his attacks.

The attacks of the *iceman*.

There is nothing quite like having a person scream because of their worst fears.

Just like I screamed as a boy, when my father beat me within an inch of my life.

No...don't go there. You have things to do.

#

It didn't take long before someone came along, people nowadays are so predictable.

He was a wino, and Milo despised winos.

Milo waited as the wino wandered drunkenly past, at the right moment he sprang at him put his hand round his mouth and slashed the back of his legs behind his knee rendering both his legs completely useless, he then tried to struggle out by punching wildly at Milo's face but he was used to this behavior and hit him at the back of the head with the blunt part of his knife and the wino was knocked out cold.

Milo dragged him across the dark blacktop and in to the sewer drain, not caring about his wound becoming septic it would just be more suffering for him in the long run.

Then he went to work on him with the knife blade, as the blood curdling screams pierced the night.

The next morning he awoke to the hideous screaming, in his head, and soon fell asleep to see it as a lullaby now.

#

He had to get some supplies and mock the world by reading the newspaper, nobody had yet caught a glimpse of his face yet, well, that have lived at least. So he was free to walk around in public. He went into the village store.

His story was on the front page and what he saw quite shocked him. *Ha-ha,* he thought, *useless cops couldn't catch a cold, belittling me saying that I might have psychological problems and shouldn't be deemed worthy for modern society.* He would love to catch the guy responsible for this and show him what *real* psychological problems could be like.

#

Back at the motel room, Milo sat watching HBO again. There was a move playing about a mafia hitman.

The so called "hitman" was nothing more than some young, baby faced punk who couldn't act worth shit and would no doubt be nominated for an award for their so called performance.

Laughing it off, he lit a cigarette and sipped some beer and turned the TV off, becoming bored with it again, and sat down at the table and opened a bottle of single malt scotch. He didn't see any reason he shouldn't enjoy the better things in life, at least for now.

He noticed he wasn't feeling bored at that point in time, either – luckily for some poor innocent slob out there, who didn't know just how lucky they really were, on the long road to nowhere.

#

But after so many weeks went by, Milo knew that he would eventually have to resurface again, for good, this time, and move on with his life, regardless of the possible repercussions.

He wanted to see his kids, too, regardless of Barbara's interference.

Nobody told the *iceman* what he could or could not do, unless they wanted to sign their own death certificate.

As it turned out, he had decided to resurface just at the right time.

#

He was lying in bed smoking a cigarette when his pager went off.

He grabbed the pager from the nightstand, to see a number he hadn't seen in a long time. His old friend from childhood, Sammy Lavano.

He didn't want to use his room phone, so he

walked down to the motel office payphone, and dialed Sammy's number from memory. After several rings, Sammy's voice. *Hey, big guy.*

Milo said, *Damn, Sammy, it's good to hear your voice again.*

Sammy said, *Ditto. What's up with you?*

Milo said, *Taking a well deserved break. And you?*

Sammy said, *I hope you can take a break from your break. I have a problem.*

Milo said, *You know me, Sammy. If the price is right, I'm in.*

Sammy said, *Good. There's this asshole, by the name of Paul. You know who I mean.*

Milo said, *As in Castelano?*

Sammy said, *One in the same.*

Milo said, *You want him dead. That's going to be expensive.*

Sammy said, *I know, but it will make John happy.*

Milo said, *As in Gotti?*

Sammy said, *You got it, big guy. You are going to be richer than ever now.*

That's exactly what Milo wanted to hear.

#

The hit was going to take place at Sparks Steak House, Paul's favorite restaurant. Paul ate there often, like clockwork, which would make it much easier for Milo to stick with the plan, no long hours of watching the place, no pissing in coffee cups or in alleyways. *A piece of cake*, as Ray would have said.

Milo's job was to take out the bodyguard, while

three other guys took out Paul, which made it even easier for him now, and still get paid thirty large for his trouble. It couldn't have been better for him – although he would have preferred to take out Paul by himself, scoring even more brownie points with John Gotti.

Sammy told him he'd have a walkie talkie to carry with him too, in case of a change in plans, an unforseen emergency. Sammy also told Milo to use a *big* gun – like a .357 – to do the job, blow the bodyguard's fucking head apart. He is *big*, Sammy said, so use caution. Milo said, *He won't even see me coming.*

Sammy believed him.

#

The next day was a cold one, overcast, gloomy – but would be even more gloomy for Paul within the next few minutes.

Milo sat across the street and half way down the block in a borrowed van, watching the front door of the restaurant. Nearby, sitting in a nondescript black Sedan, were Milo's accomplices, waiting patiently for Paul's arrival as well.

It wasn't long before Paul's car pulled up out front, with his bodyguard, Tom Bilotti, in the driver's seat, with Paul in the back, puffing on a big dog turd cigar. Milo had always hated those big cigars. Paul thought the expensive cigars had an air of class about them, but Milo thought they smelled like horse shit. If someone lit one up close to him, they'd be lucky if he didn't cram it down their throat.

After a few moments, with neither man exiting the car, Milo's walkie talkie crackled to life. An unfamiliar voice said, *Now, do it now. We don't have all fucking day. Take the bodyguard out NOW.*

Milo exited the van quickly, walking over to the car and seeing Bilotti reading the local newspaper, pulled out the .357 and fired three shots right through the paper, blowing Bilotti's head apart.

As Paul emerged from the car and turned to run, the other two assassins were there in a flash, emptying their guns into him, blowing him to pieces. Within seconds of the killings, all three assassins had already disappeared into the confused crowd of people on the street, vanishing like ghosts, nobody the wiser. Milo left alone, as always, the loner, preferring to stay that way, it was safer that way for him to remain anonymous.

He turned to look back every now and then, making sure he wasn't being followed, the gun still in his hand, as if daring anyone to tail him, so he could blow their brains out, too.

After he arrived back at the motel, after having a nice quiet, pleasant dinner, he sat back and watched TV for a while, the local news, a news bulletin about Paul and his bodyguard being gunned down in cold blood, in broad daylight, and the killers got away clean.

He couldn't help but smile.

#

Just as promised, Sammy had dropped by the next day, with Milo's thirty grand.

They had toasted the occasion with some single malt sotch, Sammy had left, and Milo sat on his bed, running his fingers through the money like it was rich green grass, soft and pleasant on his fingertips.

Then he sipped more scotch, smoked a cigarette, and began packing his belongings for his next adventure – a heartfelt attempt at reconciling with Barbara.

The very thought of it made him pour another glass of scotch.

After two more shots of liquid courage, he walked down to the office payphone to call Barbara.

It seemed like it took forever for her to answer, and when she did, she said, glumly, *Yeah?*

Milo said, *Wow, are we in a bad mood?*

She said, *You would be in a pissy mood too, if you were in my shoes.*

He said, *What's wrong now?*

She said, *Hmm...let's see. Well, I put the house up for sale, there's that. The girls and I are living with my mother, there's that, too.*

He said, *Why in the hell did you put the house up for sale?!*

She said, *What else was I supposed to do, without your dirty money?*

He said, *It's NOT dirty money, I earned it fair and square.*

She said, *I bet you did. Where have you been staying? I bet you have a mistress, most career criminals have one.*

He said, *You know better than that.*

She said, *Do I? Oh, and my mother said don't bother dropping by, you're not welcome here.*

Then she hung up.

#

Back at the room, Milo felt defeated.

He'd lost his home, his wife, and possibly his children.

But he was rich.

But he was living in a motel room.

But he was sure Sammy would have more jobs for him.

But, that mind of exposure might place a price on his head, too.

He made sure the door was locked, laid down on the bed, smoked a cigarette, and closed his eyes, hoping he could get some sleep.

Three hours later, he was still awake.

#

By daylight, he had slept about four hours.

As he climbed out of the shower, he could hear his pager going off.

It was Sammy.

He dressed quickly and walked down to the office payphone to call him. Sammy said, *Hey, big guy. Got some good news for you.*

Milo said, *I could use some good news for a change.*

Sammy said, *What's wrong?*

Milo said, I*t's the wife. She wants a divorce, and the house is up for sale.*

Sammy said, *Oh man, I'm so sorry, big guy, really I am.*

Milo said, *So, what's the good news?*

Sammy said, *The big guy, John, he really liked*

the good report on you, with the Castellano hit. He wants to use you again, soon.

Milo said, *How much does it pay?*

Sammy said, *Fifty grand.*

Milo said, jokingly, *Damn. Who does he want me to kill, the President?*

Sammy said, *Are you feeling up to some company? We need to talk about this in person.*

You know where to find me, Milo said, and hung up.

#

Sammy and Milo sat across from each other at the small table, sipping scotch.

Glancing around, Sammy said, *Damn, big guy. I'd be depressed if I lived here. No offense intended.*

Milo sipped his drink and said, *None taken. But like I said, I've been laying low for now.*

Sammy said, *Well, I can fix your problem.*

Milo said, *So, what's the job?*

Sammy said, *Have you ever heard of Gino Novelli?*

Milo said, *Can't say I have. Who is he?*

Sammy said, *He's one of the only dedicated associates of Paul Castellano left alive and breathing – at least for now.*

Milo said, *He sounds like a dedicated idiot.*

Sammy said, *He's got a big mouth, too. If the cops picked him up, he'd probably sing like a fucking canary, if it would save his own ass.*

Milo said, *Sounds like that canary needs his beak shut.*

Sammy said, *As soon as possible.*

Milo said, *So, fifty grand, huh?*

Sammy said, *Twenty-five up front, the other half when it's done.*

Milo said, *Deal. Just give me the necessary info, you know the drill.*

Sammy said, *I've got to run to the market, the wife is making homemade spaghetti sauce tonight. I'll drop the info off after dinner.*

Milo said, *Bring me a plate, I haven't had a home cooked meal in a while.*

Sammy said, *You got it.*

#

But Sammy never showed up.

Milo waited for hours, but Sammy was a no-show, not even a phone call.

Milo waited until almost midnight, thinking, *Well, I know Sammy. He got busy with dinner, and he'll be by in the morning.*

He sipped a glass of scotch and went to bed, and was asleep in minutes. He felt good about this job.

That is, until he woke up hearing someone tinkering around with the door lock.

He had acute hearing, like a big jungle cat, and the sound woke him up almost immediately. Someone trying to pick the door lock.

Someone who wasn't very good at it.

He was up from the bed in seconds, as agile as a cat, grabbinf his .38 from the night stand. He placed a silencer on the end of the barrel, and walked slowly toward the door, taking a look through the little peep hole on the door.

All he could see was a shadow; the would-be intruder had popped the light bulb above the door.

Milo stood back, aimed the barrel at the peep hole, and fired two shots.

Then he yanked the door open to see a short, stocky man dressed in black camo lying on his back, on the concrete, with a large pool of blood forming underneath his head.

In one hand he held a .45 automatic equipped with a silencer – although the mystery man wouldn't need it now.

Milo grabbed the gun from his hand, slipped it into his waistband, the used his free hand to grab the man by the foot and drag him down around the corner of the building, in the dark, and rolled the body down into a ravine behind the motel.

With the body now disposed of, he had one thing left to do before vacating his current residence.

Call Sammy.

#

Sammy answered on the second ring. *Damn, big guy. It's kind of late, don't you think?*

Milo said, *Yeah, it's too late for us.*

Sammy said, *What the hell are you talking about?*

Milo said, *Don't play dumb, Sammy. First you don't show up, then some goon shows up to kill me.*

Sammy said, *I don't know what you're talking about, Milo.*

Milo said, *You piece of shit. I should come over there right now, and cut your throat, let your wife watch me do it.*

After a few moments of silence, Sammy said, *You asshole. I should have killed you myself, when I had the chance.*

Milo said, *Yeah, you should have. Now I'm coming for YOU.*

Before Sammy could retort, Milo hung up. He had some packing to do before he vanished into the night, once again, like a ghost.

#

An hour later, as he drove around looking for another suitable motel, he couldn't help but wonder, *WHY?*

Why would a life long friend set him up with a job, then set him up to die?

Money, he thought. *It's always money.*

He drove on, day drreaming about how he was going to kill Sammy.

#

Right before daylight, after checking into another motel, he parked the Cadillac behind the building, so he wouldn't attract any unwanted attention.

Afterward, he went into his room, locked the door, pulled the window blinds shut, and began unpacking his belongings before taking a cat nap.

He didn't want to sleep too long; he had someone to *kill.*

#

He woke up around ten am, ate a quick breakfast, and sat down to listen to his portable radio.

Sure enough, he heard a broadcast about a man being found dead in a ravine. Two kids had been night fishing in the creek nearby, and found the body, called the police.

Great, Milo thought, taking a sip of scotch. *When am I going to learn, stop leaving a trail of dead bodies a mile long behind me?*

But not yet; I have to pay Sammy a visit first.

Milo knew Sammy's home was well guarded, and the guards were equipped with with *big* guns. He knew he'd have to catch him *away* from home, or at least outside, in the driveway.

He needed a high powered rifle with a scope.

And he knew just where to find one.

#

Word on the street had it that there was a new guy in the old neighborhood, name was Dom. Short for Dominique, Milo was guessing. Probably Italian, and a made man by the mob. Word was, this guy, he could get you anything you wanted, as far as weaponry was concerned; rifles, hand guns, knives, hand grenades, or even a bazooka, if you wanted one.

Problem was, how he could contact Dom, *without* being too obvious about it, put his own ass in the line of fire.

Who could he trust, to relay a message on the street?

Nobody.

Milo would have to take a ride, at night, and stake out some of the local "hot spots" around Jersey, where he knew other criminals would congregate.

He knew he could eventually find him, and, when he did, knew he could also get a good *feel* for him, if he could trust him or not. If not? He'd just add another body to his long list of victims.

Simple enough.

He took another sip of scotch, placed his .38 under his pillow, and took another cat nap.

#

He woke up around dusk.

After a long hot shower, he sat at the small table in his room, planning his first move in contacting Dom.

He knew that a lot of guys who used to be in his so called, "social circle" were regular patrons of the Kitty Kat Bar, a gentlemen's club located on the main drag.

It was a literal hot bed for criminals, so he decided to hit it first, then move on from there if need be.

He arrived at the club around eight pm, before the place was packed, to inquire about Dom. As two scantily clad ladies danced around on the stage nearby, rehearsing, Milo walked up to the bar and said to the bartender, *I wonder if you help me out. I'm trying to locate a friend of mine.*

The bartender, a tall, buzzcut guy with military tatoos on both arms, said, *Who's your friend?*

Milo said, *His name is Dom. Heard of him?*

The bartender smiled and said, *Oh yeah, crazy*

Dom. That guy, he's a real hoot. Tells all sorts of wild stories.

Milo said, *What kind of stories?*

The bartender said, *I'm guessing he used to be in the military. He told us a story once, about this guy owed him money on a drug deal gone bad. He said he pulled the pin on a hand grenade, tossed it down the guy's pants, and took off running. He heard a loud Boom! And turned around to see the poor bastard was blown in half.*

Milo said, grinning, *Sounds like my Dom. How do I get ahold of him? I haven't seen him in years.*

The bartender said, *I don't know where he lives, but he comes in here about every night around midnight, sits in that corner booth back there with his buddies.*

Milo said, *Would you give him a mesaage for me?*

With a big smile, the bartender said, *Well, sure.*

Milo pulled a small notepad and a pen from his shirt pocket, scribbled something down on the piece of paper, and handed it to the bartender. He said, *This is the number for the motel I'm staying at.*

The bartender said, *Okay, I'll give it to him as soon as he comes in.*

Turning to leave, Milo said, *I appreciate it.*

As he walked away, the bartender called after him, saying, *Who should I say wants to talk to him?*

Milo grinned and said, *Just tell him, the most evil bastard alive wants to chat with him. He'll know who I am.*

#

Around one am, as Milo sat watching HBO, the room phone rang.

He took a deep breath, answered it, and said, *Yeah?*

A deep voice on the other end said, *I hear you want to chat with me.*

Milo said, *Is this Dom?*

The voice said, *The one and only. I know who you are.*

Milo said, *Oh yeah? How's that?*

Dom said, *I've been hearing shit about you on the street, some good, some bad. What is it you want to chat about?*

Milo said, *I hear you can get your hands on just about any type of weapons I might want.*

Dom said, *You heard right. What kind of weapon are you talking about?*

Milo said, *A high powered rifle, and a scope.*

Dom said, *I got a nice, Winchester ninety-four, it goes for three hundred. The scope will be an extra fifty.*

Milo said, *Sounds good.*

Dom said, *Can I ask you a personal question?*

Milo said, *I don't see why not.*

Dom said, *Why the heavy weaponry? You could just sneak up behind them, cut their throat. A lot more quiet, and less messy.*

Milo said, *Because I want it to be messy. I want this rat to suffer.*

Dom said, *You can kill a rat with all sorts of shit. There's arsenic, cyanide. I can get you just about any liquid or powder that will do the trick.*

Milo perked up at the mention of cyanide. He

said, *You can get me cyanide? How much?*

Dom said, *How much does it cost, or in what amount?*

Milo said, *Both.*

Dom said, *It will be a lot cheaper than a rifle. I can get you enough cyanide to kill twenty rats, for a hundred bucks.*

Milo said, *Why so cheap?*

Dom said, *Because I have a good line on it. It's easy for me to get ahold of, not much time and effort goes into it, so I pass the savings on to my customers.*

Thinking it over, Milo said, *Sounds good. When can we meet up?*

Dom said, *I'll call you back at this number before noon tomorrow.*

Then Dom hung up.

Milo hung up and sipped his scotch, then took a cat nap.

#

Milo woke up around daylight, too a quick shower, and waited for Dom to call.

Dom called around ten-thirty, and said, *You know the little diner out on route six? The one with the big donut on the sign?*

Milo said, *Oh yeah, I've been there a few times.*

Dom said, *Meet me there around noon.* Then he hung up. Milo liked that; short and sweet phone calls, and all business.

He liked this Dom guy already.

#

Milo arrived early, nibbling on a donut and sipping black coffee. A few minutes later, an older model Chevy Malibu pulled up in the parking lot, and parked right outside the big bay windows.

A short, sturdily built man with short cropped black hair and a mustache exited the car and walked inside, glancing around, and fixing his eyes on Milo, walked over to the booth he was sitting in and said, *Damn, you are a big guy.*

Milo grinned and said, *I've heard that.*

Dom sat down across from Milo and said, *You're actually eating one of these donuts? You couldn't pay me enough to eat one.*

Milo said, *What's wrong with the donuts?*

Dom leaned in close and said, *All of the sugar and shit in those things? Might as well order a heart attack.*

Milo smiled and said, *I'll live.*

Dom said, *I hope so, I'd hate to lose a potential customer.*

Milo said, *Speaking of which, let's talk about the powder.*

Dom said, *Bad news, big guy. I could only get fifty bucks worth. Is that good enough for now?*

Milo said, *I've known you less than five minutes, and I have already gotten a discount. Sure, it's fine.*

Dom said, *Good deal. Now, when do you want delivery?*

Milo said, *As soon as possible.*

Dom said, *How about back here, tonight, in the back parking lot?*

Milo said, *What time?*

Dom said, *Eight o'clock?*

Milo said, *Works for me.*

Dom stood up and extended his hand to Milo, and Milo shook it. Dom said, *See ya tonight, big guy.*

Milo shook his head and went back to sipping his coffee as Dom walked out. As he watched him go, Milo thought, *I hope this works out, I'd hate to have to kill him already.*

#

Back at the motel room, Milo sipped beer and watched HBO, to pass some time.

As he sat there, watching a movie he wasn't even interested in watching, he couldn't help but wonder how his luck seemed to be improving so easily, right out of the blue, like it was meant to be.

I'm NEVER this lucky, he thought, glumly. *There has to be something wrong about this.*

Could Dom be a spy? An assassin?

Could Sammy have sent him, knowing I couldn't tolerate laying low for too long?

Milo decided, at that very moment, that Dom might have to die after all.

#

Milo arrived early, and parked behind the diner, next to the dumpster, in the pitch black night.

He wanted a barrier of darkness between him and Dom, to have an advantage over him.

A few minutes later, Dom pulled in, and, after finally spotting Milo beside the dumpster, pulled up right next to him, rolled his window down, and said, *Damn, big guy. I can't even see back here. What are you, a fucking vampire?*

Milo grinned and said, *Just being careful.*

Dom said, *Well, it never hurts to be careful.* He reached into his jacket and pulled out a small plastic bag of white powder. He said, *Here ya go, big guy.*

Milo rolled down his widnow too, with his .38 resting on his lap. He reached out and took the bag in his hand, looked at it closely, and handed Dom fifty dollars. He said, *Pleasure doing business with you.*

Dom smiled and said, *Same here. You know how to get a hold of me if you need more.*

Dom started his engine and Milo said, *Leaving so soon?*

Dom said, *Gotta go pick up the wife and kids up at the mall. Then out for ice cream.*

Milo said, *You got kids?*

Dom said, *Yeah, two daughters.*

Milo said, *Same here. Two girls.*

Dom said, *Wow, we have something else in common, huh?*

Milo said, *What was the first thing we had in common?*

Dom said, *We both hate rats and want to make money.*

Milo grinned and said, *You got that right.*

Dom said, *Well, see ya later, big guy.*

As Dom pulled away, Milo said, *See ya later.*

As he watched Dom pull away, he couldn't help but feel as though he might have judged him prematurely.

He hoped so; he needed a *real* friend right now.

                                   #

Back at the motel room, Milo made himself a pastrami sandwich, popped a beer, and sat down to watch HBO.

As he sat eating the sandwich, he thought he heard the sound of a cat meowing outside, and opened the door to investigate. Sure enough, there was a tiny, scrawny stray cat in the parking lot, begging for attention and food.

Milo thought, *It's a perfect way to test the potency of the powder.* He tore off a piece of the sandwich, dipped it in the powder, and tossed it to the cat. The cat gobbled it right up, ready for more.

Milo closed the door and went to the bathroom to wash his hands. Upon returning to open the door, there was the cat, meowing up a storm and begging for more.

He thought, *That cat should have been dead by now. What the hell is going on?*

Have I been scammed?!

He tossed the cat another piece of the sandwich dipped in the powder, and watched as the cat gobbled it right up again, and showing no signs of being sick.

I HAVE been scammed, he thought, becoming furious now. *And that Italian greaseball prick has to DIE.*

                                   #

Milo sat at the small table, in the pitch black darkness of the room, chain smoking and sipping beer and day dreaming of ways to kill Dom.

First, I'll kill Dom, then, Sammy. He thought, his blood boiling in his veins. *Or vice versa. It doesn't matter which way I do it, I just want them DEAD. And, by God, they are going to SUFFER first.*

Feed them to the rats? Burn off their balls? Skin them alive? Oh yeah...I have a lot of ways to make them suffer.

But, first things first.
First, I invite Dom out for coffee, probe his brain.
Then KILL him.

#

As Milo changed clothes, there was a loud knocking at his door.

An *urgent* knocking, like he'd heard before, many years ago, when the *cops* were wanting to speak to his father about his brother's death.

Before he could even get his shoes on, the door burst inward, off of it's frame, and four men walked in, holding hand guns, trained on Milo. Three of them were cops, and the other one was Dom.

Dom smiled and said, *Hey, big guy.*

Knowing he was defeated – at least for now – Milo sighed and said, *Hey, Dom. Good job, by the way. You're a hell of an actor.*

Dom said, *So I've been told.*

Milo said, *Well, let's just get this shit over with.*

Dom stepped forward, holding some handcuffs and leg shackles, and said, *Milo Polanski, you are under arrest for murder, conspiracy to commit murder, and six weapons violations.*

Milo said, *No problem, Dom. I'll be out in three hours.*

Dom said, *We'll see about that, big guy.*

As Milo was led through the thirty-something foot concrete walkway into the back of the jail, he was immediately bombarded by scads of reporters, microphones and cameras in hand, recording every last moment of Milo's last day as a free man.

As he walked by, he was greeted with such questions as *How many people did you kill, Milo?! Or Did you really freeze dead people?!* And the best one of all, *Are you a hit-man or serial killer?*

Both, really, you could picture him saying at one point in time, with a big shit eating grin – before his whole life fell apart before his eyes.

Otherwise, he just ignored them, sure he'd be getting out soon enough.

What he didn't know was, his money – his dirty money, as his wife had referred to it – in his Swiss bank accounts had been frozen, and all of his assets seized by the FBI.

He never saw his family again.

Like a caged animal that had been free far too long and now caught in a trap, he just paced back and forth in his cell, glaring at the guards with hatred and loathing, wishing they would walk into the cell, so he could kill every last one of them.

On December 18, 1986, Milo made his first appearance in New Jersey Superior Court, and charged with nineteen felonies, including, of course, murder.

He silently cursed both Heaven and hell – and everyone in it – except his family. The thought of what he'd put them through would haunt him until his dying day.

Barbara, although she had missed her husband at first, missed the *good* Richard, was glad that he was gone from her life as time went by. She now felt an inner peace she hadn't felt in over twenty years, and life was good again.

In March of 1988, Milo was found guilty on five counts of murder, and sentenced to five consecutive life terms in prison, meaning he would not be eligible for his first parole hearing until the age of 110.

He didn't have to wait that long. In 2006, he was diagnosed with an incurable form of Kawasaki disease, a rare condition in which the blood vessels would become inflamed, which normally would lead to cardiopulmonary arrest. He was transferred to a secure wing at St Francis Medical Center in Trenton, New Jersey, where he died on March 6, 2006.

When asked if she wanted to rescind the 'do not resuscitate order' on her former husband, Barbara declined.

His remains were taken from the medical center and cremated, and the ashes buried in a pauper's grave in an undisclosed location.

The character of Milo Polanksi was based on real life mob hit man Richard Kuklinski, who was also believed to have been a serial killer. He admitted to over 100 murders, but the actual body count is believed to have been much higher.

David Boyer is a Christian, a multi-genre writer, a true crime buff, and the author of several coming of age novellas, numerous horror and scifi stories, as well as the author of numerous essays including the subjects of government corruption, Christianity, bullying, and cyber-stalking.

He lives in Vincennes, Indiana, with his cat, Holly Jean, who now serves as his copy editor by jumping on the computer keyboard when he's not looking.

Books: {Non-fiction}
True crime:
Small Town Murder: True Crime Stories From Knox County, Indiana
Murder In the Hoosier Heartland: Infamous Indiana Murderers & Fledgling Serial Killers
Murder & Mayhem In the Hoosier Heartland: Mysterious Disappearances & Bizarre Murders In Indiana
The Blitz: A Rape Victim's Story
Vanished In Vincennes: the Mysterious Disappearance and Death Of Dolores Oliver
47 Years of Hell: The Dolores Oliver Murder: Still Unsolved
Small Town Murder In Knox County, Indiana: Hate Crimes, Witch Hunts, and A Definitive List of Indiana Serial Killers
The Guy In The Blue Shirt

Non-fiction: {paranormal, bio & memoir}
Haunted Heartland: Haunted Hoosiers Tell Their Ghost Stories
Strange Happenings In the Hoosier Heartland
I Remember When, In Vincennes…Volume 1
Growing Up In Vincennes – Volumes 2 – 5
The Time of Our Lives: Growing Up Cool In Vincennes, Indiana

Essays:
Bullying: the Road to Recovery and Forgiveness
Privacy In the Age of the Internet: How Sexting and Sharing Private Photos Can lead To Cyber-Stalking
Once An Alcoholic, Always An Alcoholic? The Cold Hard Truth About Our Addictions
Travesties of Jutice: Flaws In Our Legal System That Imprison the Innocent
Will the REAL Christian Please Stand Up?
Racism in the 21st Century: ALL Lives Matter
Conflicted Souls: How the Man In Black Saved My Life
Crossing the Rainbow Bridge: Saying Goodbye To Our Beloved Pets

Books: {Fiction}
Mystery, Indiana
Human Sawdust
The Ghost In My Head
A Righteous Cop

Stories: {Long fiction, novellas}
Mystery, Indiana
The Mind of Luther Biggs

LUTHER
Jenny
Lester Talbot and His Magic Eye
Beautiful Ghosts
Pretty Flamingo
Jack and Norma Jean
The Things We Leave Behind – Volumes 1 – 3
Ghosts of Summer
Gardens
Claustrophobia
The Cemetery Artist
Brain Pie
Beast
The Jailhouse Movie Star
Easy Pickings
The Dominant Thumb
Joyride
The Maverick
Freak
Grandma's Gooseberry Pie
Dancing With the King
Always In My Heart
Hillbilly Moonshine Zombies
Home
Sheva
A Debt Repaid In Full
The Enlightening Darkness
The Good Neighbor
Wander
The Hungry Ones
A Gunfighter's Legacy
Dead Man's Hand
Inhuman Experiments – Part 1, 2, and 3

Jennifer
Spider Bait
Goodnight, My Love
Poor Larry
Creepy Crawl
The Ballad Of Georgie

Dolores Oliver, fondly nick-named 'Lert' by her friends as a term of endearment, was out an out-going and friendly woman who was well liked by all who knew her.

Yet, on September 7, 1974, while on a visit to a local bar to chat with friends, she simply vanished without a trace. Foul play was immediately suspected by her family, who knew in their hearts that they could think of absolutely no one who would want to do her any harm.

Yet her lifeless body was found at the end of October in a bean field by a farmer in Illinois. Lawrence County coroner Dale Nichols was able to make a positive ID through dental records and a ring Mrs Oliver was wearing.

Who would have done such a thing, and why? Hopefully, VANISHED IN VINCENNES will help to finally solve one of the oldest cold cases in Indiana, and bring her family some closure they have sought for so long.

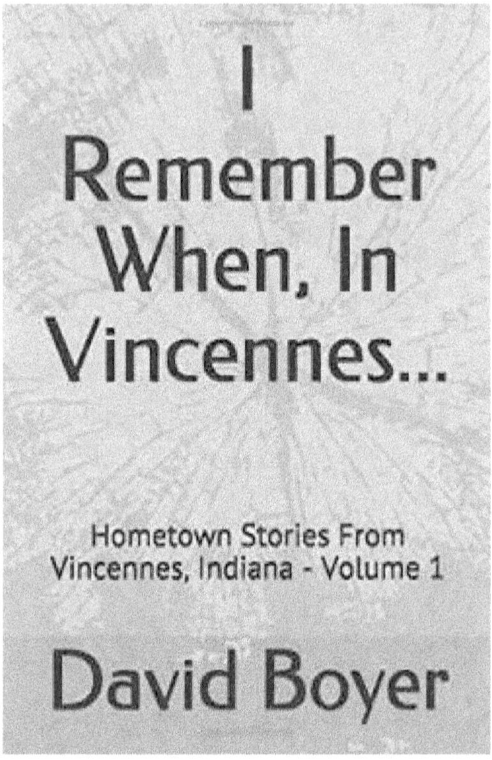

Unfortunately, even small towns – Vincennes included – eventually change, sometimes for the better, and other times, not so much. It's the natural order of things.

Trees grow old and fall. Sidewalks split and crack and are replaced for public safety's sake. Old houses – and all the memories associated with them – are demolished and replaced with parking lots or duplexes. Even historical landmarks, Mother Nature and Father Time having taken their toll, sadly, vanish – except for our own pictures and memories of them.

Luckily for Vincennes residents, local historian Norbert Brown has created a Facebook group page entitled, *Vincennes Remember When*, to help all of us keep our fond memories intact, and to reminisce and enjoy them 24-7.

It was his infinite wisdom of our local history and group page that was the inspiration for this book – and the stories within. Some of these stories may elicit a tear, some laughter.

Some may remind you of an old friend you haven't seen since high school – or, sadly, one that has passed in recent years. Some may remind you of your childhood, your teenage years – or having to bid them farewell, in order to move on to bigger and better things; marriage, children, grandchildren, and a lifetime of wonderful memories that only a tight-knit, loving family can provide.

It is my sincere belief that there will be a story for *everybody* within these pages, regardless of whether you may be a Vincennes history buff or not.

As of 2015, it is believed that there are at least 200 serial killers active in the United States at any given time.

33 of them were from Indiana.

Nobody in their own home town would have wanted to imagine a fledgling {or full fledged} serial killer lurking about, searching for his next victim. Or imagine one being their next door neighbor or the relative of a friend or even attending the local college.

Yet, since the early 1970s, Vincennes, Indiana, Knox County, and Indiana in general has had it's share of cold blooded murder.

It's really sad – as well as terrifying – to even imagine all these brutal, cold blooded murders have taken place in small town communities, where, at one time, we could all trust just about everyone we met at least to the extent they'd do us no harm; a time when could leave our doors unlocked at night or a window open for a cool breeze or not have to worry about where our children were – or if they'd ever come home again.

In SMALL TOWN MURDER, we will be examining local cases, old cases, more recent cases, and the aftermath it leaves behind for the victim's families – as well as taking an in-depth look into a deep, dark, world none of us would ever want to see – but has been here all along, and, most likely, always will be.